"I am so impressed with 'Cracking the Boy's Clu... woman dealing with men should read this boo... more cleverly, professionally and less emotion... accomplished assertiveness." Dr. Laura Schlessing... Author: "The Proper Care and Feeding of Husban...

*\*\**

"In the corporate world, where women sometimes have a steeper ladder to climb, Michael Johnson's "Cracking the Boy's Club Code" is a book of secrets men use in business and a must read for all working women. Not only will it help yc                                  ꞁg, it will show you hov Pat Dai                                     San Jose City Counci!

"Cracki          ( for women
who wc            nale business
mind ar           want without
compro
Carol K           Owners

There a           ꞁmen still lag
behind           *The Woman's*
*Guide t*          he beginning
with ou          andings and
miscom          ꞁou will have
the tool          and listened
to with          ꞁains, KGO
Radio

"*Crack*          ; dedicated
to offe          control in
their ‖          tep-by-step
ways fᴇ          ears a path
for mᴏ          K. Bolliger,
Found

# Cracking the Boy's Club Code:

*The Woman's Guide to Being Heard and Valued in the Workplace*

# Cracking the Boy's Club Code:

*The Woman's Guide to Being Heard and Valued in the Workplace*

Michael B. Johnson

New York

# Cracking the Boy's Club Code!
## The Woman's Guide to Being Heard and Valued in the Workplace

ISBN 978-1-60037-642-9

Library of Congress Control Number: 2009929149

# MORGAN · JAMES
## THE ENTREPRENEURIAL PUBLISHER

Morgan James Publishing, LLC
1225 Franklin Ave., STE 325
Garden City, NY 11530-1693
Toll Free 800-485-4943
www.MorganJamesPublishing.com

In an effort to support local communities, raise awareness and funds, Morgan James Publishing donates one percent of all book sales for the life of each book to Habitat for Humanity. Get involved today, visit www.HelpHabitatForHumanity.org.

*To my daughters, Shea and Sybil:*
*It is a privilege to be your father.*
*Without you, my life would be incomplete.*

# Contents

# Acknowledgements

Writing this book has been one of most rewarding and thought-provoking experiences I have ever undertaken. As with every worthwhile endeavor, it would not have been possible without the help, support and encouragement of many people.

First, I want to acknowledge and thank my daughters, Shea and Sybil, who have always given me their unconditional love and trust. It was through them that I began to realize just how different are the two sexes. Though it took me a long time to figure it all out, they never gave up hoping that I eventually would.

Special thanks to all of the women who graciously provided the stories you will soon read about in the following pages:

| | |
|---|---|
| Rosie Cofre | Jennifer Nickens |
| Francine Epstein | Promise Phelon |
| Ann Giluso | Laura Roden |
| Barbara Kivowitz | Laura Shenkar |
| Marci Levine | Ann Smith |
| Joanne Linden | Jeannine Nicole Walker |
| Linda McFarland | Kim Wamsley |

While the names found in the book are pseudonyms to protect confidentialities, all of the stories are from real-life situations. The stories bring to life the situations that women all over the world experience in the workplace.

The book would not be the same without the help of my illustrator, Akiko Kasuya, www.akikokasuya.mosaicglobe.com/) whose creativity and talent brought the book to life. I would also like to thank my photographer, Sean Dufrene (www.seandufrene.com) for the beautiful photographs.

I also would like to extend my thanks to the many women in my workshops who encouraged me to write this book. If it had not been for them, the book would still be a figment in my imagination!

I would like to express my eternal gratitude to the girl's mother, Laura, the giver of life. Without her, my daughters would not exist and my life incomplete beyond imagination.

Lastly, I must thank Mary Claire Blakeman, who took my manuscript and made it readable. Without her talent and incredible patience, this book would never have seen the light of day. Thank you, Mary!

And a very special thank you to Ellen Rudy of the Hayden Group (www.TheHaydenGroup.com) for the beautiful cover design.

*"We see things not as they are; we see them as we are."*
*Anais Nin*

# Introduction

I have written this book for my daughters— the sheriff and the chef—and for working women everywhere.

My 11-year marriage came to an end in 1980, and I was devastated. My ex-wife and I decided on joint custody, with the girls spending weekends with her and weekdays with me. Over time, the girls spent most weekends with me in order to be with their friends.

Here I was a single father, with two very young daughters, ages four and six. In the 1980s, single fathers were a rarity. There were no support groups (although I don't know that I would have become involved even if there were) and no "how-to" books for single dads. How could I raise my daughters to be independent, self-assured women when I wasn't able to give them an intact family like the one I had growing up?

If only they were boys, I would have had a better idea of what to do. At least I would be on somewhat familiar territory. I'd get them into sports—take them fishing and hunting—all the "manly" activities. But they were girls. I needed a different game plan. Or so I thought.

Then I met Dr. White, a child psychiatrist. Dr. White was a large and imposing man in stature, yet amazingly kind, gentle and wise in demeanor. His voice was soft and soothing. My daughters took to him immediately. After one session with us, he asked me to make an appointment with him alone.

Why would Dr. White want to see me alone? Would he tell me what I already knew; that I was a failure and completely unfit to raise my daughters? My mind worked overtime on the worst possible scenarios. I imagined he would tell me that I would have to find a good home for my daughters—like you would for unwanted pets.

The day arrived for my appointment with Dr. White. As I braced myself for the inevitable, he asked how I was doing and what questions I had about raising my girls. I answered with a long litany of all my failures. I told Dr. White I was completely responsible for my marriage failing and the resulting damage to the girls.

Dr. White listened quietly. After I had exhausted all my "mea culpas," he began: "Time for you to quit thinking of yourself and start concentrating on raising your daughters. Yes, it is true that in a perfect world, your daughters would be much better off with an intact, loving family. This is not a perfect world, and that is not the cards you were dealt. You need to reassure your girls that: they are not the reason for the divorce, they are safe and you will be there for them, and they are loved. If you do that, they will be fine. Are you up to that?"

"Of course I'm up to that!" I assured him. That was easy. After all, keeping loved ones safe is a high priority for males. But "being there" for them and letting them know they were loved came less naturally to me as a father. Merely telling my daughters I loved them was not enough. They wanted, needed and deserved much more. And so my wondrous and perplexing journey into the dynamics of male-female relationships began.

## The Sheriff

Shea and Sybil could not be more different. Shea was outgoing, very athletic and a natural with people. She was also a great salesperson. I remember when she was about seven years old; she took her sister with her as she sold out-of-date calendars to the neighbors. Her sister, Sybil, was five at the time and looked very much like a waif in one of Dickens' novels. The combination of Shea's outgoing personality and Sybil's forlorn demeanor proved irresistible to the neighbors. At the end of the day, she had made more than $5—and that was in the early 1980s!

Shea also had a fascination with incarceration at a very young age. There were many times when I would hear one of her friends or her sister screaming—only to find them either locked in a room or in plastic handcuffs begging to be freed. Today, Shea is a sheriff. I am proud to say that she is the youngest person, male or female, to be promoted to sergeant in the history of her department!

**The Chef**
Sybil was the complete opposite of Shea, finding solace in arts, crafts, dolls, makeup, clothes and cooking. Where Shea wanted to play catch or tag football with me, Sybil wanted to help me cook, especially bake. I have always had a fascination with baking: breads, pastries, pies and desserts. Sybil was my shadow in the kitchen. Her favorite thing was to put on apron, stand on a stool and help me make cookies. Today, in addition to mothering her two sons, Sybil is a pastry chef with her own specialty baking enterprise.

**Girls and Boys Are Different**
Raising my two daughters (or were they raising me!) has given me a deep appreciation for just how much alike—and how very different—the two sexes are. Not in terms of physical attributes and proclivities but the way women and men *view* their world.

The differences in the sexes were manifested in the lives of my daughters as they matured, especially during their teenage years. "I hate him." "Why can't he just...." "He is so lame!" These were common refrains in our household. Long talks about boys and how they think were constant topics of our discussions, both with my girls and their friends.

Many times one of my daughters would come to me frustrated or hurt about a transgression she suffered from a "lame" male friend who had treated her poorly. Invariably when I inquired about what had happen was I discovered the offending male had treated my daughter as he would...another boy. The boy probably liked my daughter and thought her was paying her a compliment!

Parenting my daughters, I taught them how to defuse conflicts and gave them the tools they would need to win in the world of work and in life. With this book, my aim is to share my experience and perspective as a male with women who want to work, play and grow with men. (My next book *will be* for men!)

In the following chapters, we will look at the evolutionary forces that have shaped men's thinking and some not-yet-surfaced rules by which men live. Once women understand how men view the world and how that view shows up in their behavior, they will be able to more effectively communicate with—and influence—men.

Indeed, my hope is that they both enjoy more success and less stress in their jobs, careers and personal lives.

# My Daughters Today

Shea, my oldest, shown here in this recruitment poster, is responding to a real-life hostage situation. She is frequently called in to negotiate such situations owing to her non-threatening and nurturing manner; reducing the risk of injury to hostage, the perpetrator and the police. We will see how femininity combined with firmness (not aggression) is a winning strategy with males. This is the reason Shea is called in. (Photo: The perpetrator released the hostage and was taken peacefully into custody.)

Sybil, my youngest, is a pastry chef who works in some of San Francisco's finest restaurants, including Aqua. She and her husband have two sons. In addition to being a full-time mom, she runs her own successful catering service, specializing in fine pastries, cakes and desserts.

# Chapter 1: The Caveman in the Corner Office

How is it that men can forget an angry confrontation when it's over—yet a woman can re-hash that same incident again and again?

Why is it that so many women seem capable of doing three things at once—while men typically like to handle only one item at a time?

And why is it still so difficult for men and women to understand each other, even in this age of communicating, connecting with cell phones, email and text messaging?

These questions about the differences between men and women can be answered, in my opinion, by examining the traits that have been handed down to us all by our earliest ancestors: *Homo sapiens*.

Though we may not be consciously aware of them, the strategies and behaviors that enabled our cavemen and women ancestors to survive have been encoded—or "hard wired"—into our brains, and they continue to influence how we speak and act today.

Let me explain—and possibly shed some light on the questions posed above. Our caveman forebearers hunted animals for food, for survival, which meant they had to stay focused on one single thing—killing the prey. Had they let themselves become distracted or tried to multi-task during a hunt, they could have been killed by an animal. After a brutal battle with wild animals, the men of the hunting party had to forget the pain they endured in the fight— else they would have feared going out and hunting. Had that been their habit, all would have starved.

In today's versions of those scenarios, businessmen often prefer reading bullet points that cover only one subject at a time, instead of detailed, descriptive emails on multiple topics. Guys in the office might all go out for a beer together after work, even if they've had a confrontational screaming match earlier in the day.

So in your workplace, you can often see men using updated versions of the same tactics that cavemen depended on to survive. When you begin to recognize how evolutionary events of the past have made us who we are today, you have a better chance of deciphering and understanding what's going on with the males you work and live with. You will also be in a much stronger position to communicate effectively with both men and women. *And that is the goal of this book: to make you a better communicator.*

Now, by drawing a connection between the behavior of the caveman and the attitudes of the twenty-first century businessman, I do not mean to imply that all men are brutes or that uncivilized behavior should be tolerated. Rather, I believe that both men *and* women have evolved in ways that complement each other and have allowed our species to survive and prosper. Men and women have unique strengths and weaknesses that evolution has given them. The strengths of one complement the weaknesses of the other and vice versa. When both genders respect and balance their differences, their work together becomes effortless—instead of getting bogged down in misunderstandings and miscommunication.

Going back to examine the ancient past, then, is more than an attempt to understand evolutionary psychology. It is a practical pursuit that can give you real insights into the problems you may be facing on your job or in your business. Before we travel through history to examine the specific caveman traits that continue to show up in today's workplace, it is helpful to keep these points in mind:

FIRST, any discussion in the highly-charged arena of male-female relationships runs the risk of stereotyping both genders or citing generalizations about behavior that do not apply to every single person. It is impossible to avoid that risk entirely; nevertheless, I have attempted to do so by alerting you in advance that this book is built on research and personal observations about the behavior of the *average* male and the basic *tendencies* displayed by each gender. Remember, averages, represent the middle ground between two extremes. For example, men tend to have greater upper body strength than women. This does not mean that *all* men have more upper body strength than *all* women. As you read these pages, you will no doubt think of men—or women—who do not adhere to a particular behavior pattern. Just remember that we're talking about the *tendencies* of typical males and females, not specific individuals.

SECONDLY, each gender has false assumptions about the other, and those assumptions are the source of many problems. Each of us has our own and unique view of the world. While these views may be similar to those of others, they are never identical. Yet we assume and act as if everyone else sees the world in the same way that we do. This is a mistake. As I related in the story about my daughters when they were young in the Introduction, boys often treated them in the same manner as they would treat other boys—and my girls would reject those boys as friends or playmates because of it. The boys assumed that girls perceived the world just as they did; they were shocked when their teasing and bantering backfired. Women, too, make the mistake of assuming that men share their perception of reality—experiencing being blindsided by male behavior or being angry and resentful about it. To avoid those traps and get the most from this book, I invite you to put aside your pre-conceived judgments about men, so you can be open to new insights.

THIRD, men are often not conscious about much of their behavior because they have been "acting like men" since they were four or five years old. To establish their identities as males, boys have to separate from their mothers and reject her female dimension. They start adapting to the norms of other males at such a young age that, by the time they are adults, men assume that their attitudes and behaviors simply reflect what "normal guys" think and do. This means that even though females may not have to deal with the blatant overt sexism of the past (which, granted, has not disappeared entirely), the bigger problem for most women is the unconscious—and unproductive—ways in which men relate to them. Women's business calls to men are not returned. They experience being passed over for promotions and fail to break through the infamous "glass ceiling" to advance to the highest levels of a company. For the most part, however, men in the business world are not consciously seeking to put women down or keep them from advancing. In fact, men actively look for people who can help their team win *and they do not care about gender as long as everyone contributes to winning.* Beyond that, many men are simply unaware of what they say or do that can make women feel "dissed" or left out. I bring up this point not to excuse men, but to help you understand why some guys "just don't get it," when women complain to or about them.

FINALLY, because of these differences in gender roles that began taking place hundreds of thousands of years ago, men and women have evolved in ways that virtually create two separate cultures. (See section entitled *"A Tale of Two Travelers" at the end of this chapter.*) Male business culture—which still predominates—focuses on linear, top-down hierarchies to get things done, while women tend to build more flat, web-like networks to accomplish their goals. There is no right or wrong; both have much to offer the other. To appreciate male business culture, the best strategy is to act as though you were going to work in a foreign country. In that situation, while there, you would no doubt take time to learn about the culture. You might find some of the foreigner's customs to be strange or perplexing—but if you wanted to do business in that country, you wouldn't judge, belittle or try to change them. By the same token, when you read my observations and advice about dealing with men in the workplace, you should consider this information to be a guidebook to a culture that does not operate by the same rules or codes as your own.

Instead of focusing on the flaws of male business culture, think of yourself as an anthropologist who is trying to maintain a neutral attitude about the people she is studying. As an anthropologist, one of your first tasks is to look at the history of this culture of men.

**Our Ancestors**
Approximately 200,000 years ago, scientists tell us, our earliest human ancestors, *Homo sapiens*, came on the scene. That was

some years after the era of the hominids, *Homo erectus* and Australopithecus *afarensis*, whose most famous member was "Lucy," the name given to the complete skeleton of an adult female discovered by paleontologists in 1973. (Lucy, it turns out, was named for the Beatles tune, "Lucy in the Sky with Diamonds," that was playing in the camp at the time of her discovery.)

As intriguing as Lucy and her kin were, human development became most interesting with the arrival of *Homo sapiens* (who co-existed with the *Neanderthals*, less developed than the *H. sapiens*, but hardly the knuckle-dragging dim-wits they are usually depicted as being).

For our purposes, the reason things got interesting when *H. sapiens* came on the scene was that, for the first time, there was a division of labor along gender lines. Prior to *H. sapiens,* both men and women hunted and gathered. Women and children most likely accompanied the men on hunts, helping flush game out of hiding, processing the animal, and participating in other hunting activities that did not require direct, close contact with dangerous beasts. When *H. sapiens* began to vary their diets—consuming fish, collecting wild seeds, and eating other foods—they set in motion the age of the hunter-gatherers.

Besides noting the changes in their dietary habits, archeologists have also found evidence that *sapiens* manufactured clothing and shelter, as seen in their basketry, bone awls and eyed needles. This evidence underscores the idea that *H. sapiens* divided labor based on gender and age.

In early man, sexual dimorphism (the difference in strength and body size between male and female) was much larger than it is today. Because of their larger size, men became the natural (and nature's) choice for hunting large, dangerous animals. The smaller-sized females became nature's choice to remain in the relative safety of the camp to care for the children, process and cook food, and perform essential crafts such as creating clothing, making baskets, building shelters. There was another very important reason for women to stay behind in areas that were somewhat safer: men were expendable; women were not (and you'll read more about this later in this chapter).

It was this diversified, cooperative subsistence economy that provided several very distinct advantages to *H. sapiens*. Primarily, diversification enabled *H. sapiens* to reduce the feast and famine cycles associated with large-game hunting by adding plants, tubers, fish, nuts and berries to their diets. Without this diversification, the economic cost of gathering and processing those products was prohibitive. It simply took too much time and effort to collect and break down these foods for the caloric reward they provided.

Cooperation and diversification also allowed the women to forego the hunt in order to care for children. No longer did all group members need to be in close contact during the quest for food—each gender had more opportunity to specialize. The emergence of this gendered division of labor continues to our current day and has been practiced in nearly every culture for the last 60,000 years or so. These early beginnings of specialization are both the basis for our survival—and the source of much of our misunderstandings and miscommunication with one another.

## The History of the Hunters and the Gatherers

Let's look briefly at the breeding grounds for those misunderstandings:

To be good hunters, males had to be fearless, strong and able to run for long distances. Since the prey was often large and dangerous, reliance on other members of the hunting party was paramount. The last thing a good *H. sapiens* male wanted was someone "wimping out" in the hour of need. The less contact the hunter had with the prey, the safer he was. That fact led to a strong desire to develop sophisticated weapons, snares and other tools that would enable the hunter to kill at a distance.

Males, therefore, became focused on *things*—specifically things that would help them in the hunt. They also studied the habits of indigenous animals, the location of watering holes, and the best methods for capturing and killing prey, as well as improvements in designs for new weapons and hunting tactics. The more the males could control their environment, the better their chance for bringing home food.

Males became obsessed with understanding how their environment worked and how they could manipulate it in their favor. They were driven to systematize and solve problems. Does this sound familiar? Do any of the men you know act that way? Do you have a male toddler who is obsessed with taking things apart with maddening regularity or putting small objects (marbles, coins, parts of a toy) into places they don't belong (dryer, heat register, nose)? This drive to create systems and seek solutions is in the nature of males and is programmed into every one of us guys at the unconscious level. (So now you know why your husband or significant other may jump in to try to solve your problems, when all you want him to do is listening to what's going on in your life.)

The rewards for improving their ability to kill wild game went beyond simply gathering food to eat. Good hunters also received another very important perk: access to females. In early times, the most aggressive and successful male had the most access to females and other spoils of winning. After all, he had proved to be the best provider and protector for the group.

Having access to females was no small achievement for the males. On a deep level, (all the way down to the cellular level some scientist would say), primitive man was driven to pass on his genes and insure the survival of his bloodline through children. While every member of the group had some value in terms of survival, males were more expendable because one male could impregnate many women. Females, by contrast, were not biologically expendable. Her reproductive years were limited and the time needed to care for and raise her children was considerable compared to other primates. Therefore, the death of one female had severe repercussions on the survival of the group. Those expendable males, however, could be sent out to do the more dangerous job of hunting—should one or a few of them end up in the belly of a tiger, the tribe would still survive. The males who were not the big winners in the hunt did not get access to women, so their DNA died out.

Are you beginning to get the idea of why modern men still jockey for position when they're with a group of other men, or always have to establish who's in the "top dog" position? And can you begin to see how men would express those old primal drives in business where they must *hunt* for ideas (or customers), *chase* after solutions, *capture* contracts and make sure everyone knows the *aim* of their companies.

As for the females, the gender-based specialization of labor developed by *H. sapiens* also governs the behaviors we see in women today. Because of pregnancy and giving birth (and eventual child-care duties), our female ancestors were at risk. During pregnancy, the woman was less able to participate in the more strenuous duties of daily living in *H. sapiens* society. It was not that these women were weak; rather, as noted above, protection of the fetus was vitally important for the survival of the group. If a mother became ill or injured, she had to rely on the other women in the group to help care for her and her child.

While the males were off hunting, it was only through the help of the group that the females could protect themselves from dangers posed by an aggressive male from another clan or a large predator. In the animal kingdom, researchers have found many examples of female apes and chimpanzees (our closest relative) that protect each other and their offspring by attacking an intruder en masse.

Females, then, became dependant on each *other* to survive. The women focused on *people* and not on *things*. Because help from others was vital to survival, it was imperative that each female keep close tabs on their relationships with the other females. Grooming, vocalization, reading verbal and body clues gave indications as to their closeness (dependability) with others in the group. In extreme cases, the loss of a close relationship with her group meant banishment and certain death for her and/or her offspring. On the other hand, by maintaining those close relationships, the *H. sapiens* mother heightened the chances that other mothers would care for her children if she died or was killed; whereas the males would not, for the most part, protect the child of another male.

You gather, from this short examination of our common ancestry, the potential for the conflicting priorities of men and women. The males focused on status, the females on relationships; the males depended on their brute strength and weapons to protect them, the women counted on other women to come together for mutual protection. For men today, the loss of *status* can be devastating (and emotionally equivalent to death as his chances to pass on his genes are reduced)—while for women, the loss of *relationships* can be akin to an emotional death, echoing the real death our female ancestors would experience if they were banished by the women of the group.

Of course, reducing human behavior to primal instincts may seem to ignore the issue of free will and choice. I would argue, however, that we each make choices based on whether we see the world through the eyes of the hunter or the gatherer. The hunter sees the world as things that work according to a set of rules that he must learn to navigate, a world ruled by the quest for status and power. The gatherer sees the world as relationships with people that must be nurtured and maintained.

I firmly believe that the more each gender understands the other's view of the world, the more respect and understanding there can be; which can only result in better communication and higher productivity for everyone.

To help you understand the ancient hunter's perspective; that is, the unconscious, underlying perspective of modern males; I have identified several of the most important traits or skills he needs to succeed in his world. In upcoming chapters, these characteristics are discussed in further depth. For now, this brief overview will describe traits of the ancient hunter that you need to recognize and cope with in your modern work environment.

## Hallmarks of a Hunter

To avoid being thrown off the back of a huge elk or wooly rhinoceros, breaking his neck, and ending his life sooner than the short 30 years he might possibly live, *Homo sapiens* hunters had to be fast, agile and strong.

## A good hunter also had to be able to:

### *Stay silent and focused on a single objective*

Men would spend long hours searching for the prey, looking for telltale signs of its movement, or waiting silently for the animal to travel along a familiar route. Intense concentration—with no time for chitchat—was required, because he might have only a single chance to land the killing blow. Hunters also communicated in silence, through gestures. In Chapter 2, you will learn how this emphasis on staying single-focused and silent affects communication with men in business and how it can clash with the multi-tasking style of some women in the workplace.

### *Fight to be the best*

The more successful the *H. sapiens* hunter, the more power and respect he received—and the more food and females were his, also. No wonder, then, that ancient males and modern men alike engage in constant struggles for power and status, sometimes subtly and good-naturedly and other times in bare-knuckled fashion. Chapter 3 helps women understand how to maneuver around the inevitable games of male one-upmanship in the workplace without getting caught up in game.

### *Forget the fight*

When males fight for dominance, they rarely do so "to the death." Once the pecking order is established and the fight is over, it's over. Men have the capacity (and the type of brains) that allows them to move on after a confrontation, and Chapter 4 explains that phenomena and its implication for women.

### *Take risks*

Given that survival was literally at stake, *H. sapiens* men had to take risks and distinguish themselves in the hunt to reap the rewards that followed. Women, who were responsible for bearing and raising the children and whose survival was paramount for the group, had less incentive to run risks. In Chapter 5, you will gain further insights into risk-taking and learn how men get points just for trying, whether or not their risk ever pays off.

### *Manipulate things*

Being able to heave the right type of rock at exactly the right time to bring down a charging animal could save the life of a hunter in pre-historic times. Being able to implement the right type of software program to eliminate cost overruns could save the job of a modern-day manager. The discussion in Chapter 6 is designed to help you understand the male priority of putting *things* first—before people or relationships—so that you can be more effective in setting and communicating *your* business priorities.

### *Respect the rules*

Sports and games replicate many aspects of the ancestral hunt, such as chasing, capturing, or smashing a ball (the weapon) into the goal (prey). Men, who at heart love to systematize, view rules as sacrosanct and strive to establish clear winners and losers—even though they may be simultaneously on the lookout for loopholes that can circumvent those rules. Women, who tend to approach games and play from a completely different angle than men, need to understand male attitudes on this subject. Chapter 7 explains them.

### *Make sure your hunting party is victorious*

Pre-historic males had to rely completely on the other members of their hunting party—*their team.* After all, if you were going to leap onto the back of an irate rhino, you wanted to make sure the others were on hand to quickly dispatch the animal. To the hunters, it didn't matter if they liked each other very much, as long as they could rely on the other men in times of stress. Chapter 8 gives women more insight into this male style of working together that is different from the relationship-centered style with which they may be more comfortable.

### My hope for you

While evolution was imprinting behavioral differences on the Hunter and the Gatherer, the brains of men and women also developed along divergent paths as well. Throughout the book, in addition to learning how the traits of the Hunter still operate in business, you will also find tidbits of information on "Brain Basics" to help you understand how the very structure of each gender's brain creates some of the communication problems men and women experience.

As you read, you will also learn practical communication strategies that you can put into use in your relationships with men, whether in your professional—or personal—life. My intent for you is that by the time you finish this book you will be a stronger and more confident communicator.

I also hope that you will come to the one realization that can serve you, no matter what you do in life, and that realization is this: *It's not personal!* The things that other people say really do not mean anything about you. Their reactions are simply that— reactions to something that was triggered within them. You are merely witnessing their drama! When you begin to understand where men (and women) are coming from, you will be able to step back and realize that their comments and assessments represent their best efforts to communicate, and it is really not "personal." Once you can incorporate that insight into your thinking, you will find it takes the sting out of day-to-day interactions. Then you have a true choice about how you respond, and you are also truly free to understand other human beings.

## A Tale of Two Travelers

Imagine two businesswomen who are each preparing for an important meeting in a foreign country. Elizabeth spends her time studying business objectives and polishing her presentation. She is an expert in her field and knows the proposal backwards and forward. If anything, she is *over* prepared. She is leaving nothing to chance—or so she thinks.

Karen also studies the company's objectives and practices her presentation. But Karen goes one step further than Elizabeth. She takes the time to understand the culture of her foreign customer.

Through her research, Karen learns that getting down to business right away is considered rude in that client's culture. Business is never conducted until both parties have had time to get to know one another through drinks, meals and golf. In fact, in the client's country, 80 percent of success is determined by how well this "getting-to-know-you" period is handled.

Once this stage is completed, the client is ready to talk about the business at hand. Again there are specific unwritten rules about how each subject is broached, who will bring up certain issues, and when they will be addressed. Karen knows that to violate these unwritten rules will be seen as a danger sign to the client, and a signal that the offender cannot be trusted.

Armed with this knowledge of how the client expects business to proceed, Karen is able to earn both the trust and respect of her foreign partners and is rewarded with a large contract and a relationship that endures over time.

Contrast this with Elizabeth, who understands the business aspects of the meeting as well as, if not better than, Karen— yet she has not bothered to understand the customs of the client. After all, she muses, "People are people… their second language is English… this is a global market… and how different could they really be from me?"

As you probably can guess, as soon as Elizabeth's plane lands, she is raring to go. She suggests that everyone meet at 8 a.m. the next day to go over her presentation. The client is taken aback. Who is this person! Why is she treating us this way? Doesn't she respect us? Although not her intent, Elizabeth has shown her prospective clients that, indeed, she does not care about them. She only cares about herself.

While the client did not verbalize any disfavor, the outcome is doomed. This business relationship will go nowhere. Elizabeth, oblivious to her situation, continues with her presentation while the client politely listens, having no intention to act upon any of her suggestions.

After the meeting has ended, everyone smiles and nods approvingly, and Elizabeth believes she has won a new client. Little does she realize that this will be the last time she talks with this client again.

Far fetched? "This would never happen to me!" you may be thinking. "I know better than to approach a foreign client without learning about how to do business in that country."

Yet every day, you may be acting just like Elizabeth when doing business with people from another culture: men.

Male business culture has any number of hidden, coded and unwritten rules that govern it. Men grow up knowing this; women often do not. Women find out about them when they somehow transgress a rule and then suffer the consequences—a deal doesn't go through, a promotion gets denied, a phone call is never returned. So, just as you would adopt a neutral, pragmatic stance in studying the culture of a foreign business client, so, too, do you need to learn about the rules and rituals the opposite sex follows in business. If you don't, chances are high that your results will be similar to those of Elizabeth.

## Chapter 2: One Thing at a Time

In the second week of her new job, Jocelyn arrived at the office before 8 a.m. and got busy writing an email to her boss. She wanted to be sure to tell him everything he might need to know about the meeting he'd asked her to set up. Her fingers flew across the keyboard as she wrote:

*Dear Howard,*
*I have had to contact Dave and his team to get clearance, and also talked to Sharon in Operations, and Jack in Sales to make sure there won't be any problems with setting up your meeting to discuss the new strategic plan that you outlined when you had your meeting with Tom back in February during the push to re-organize the division and re-establish the priorities for next year. Sharon has no problem with our using the west conference room, but Jack prefers the one on the north side of the building because the room doesn't get as hot. I told him that you like the room on the west side because the view is so spectacular and he said that would be okay also…*

Just then the phone rang and Jocelyn hit the "save" button on her computer to make doubly sure she wouldn't lose any of the precious words she'd taken so much care to write…

You may be glad that phone rang because otherwise, you might have had to read the rest of Jocelyn's lengthy email. It might not surprise you to know that her boss never got around to reading all of it either.

Even though Jocelyn waited most of the day for a response from Howard, all he could muster was a shrug, telling her he "hadn't gotten to it yet" when she asked him about the email. By the end of the day, he curtly told Jocelyn good night and headed to the elevator and out of the building. Jocelyn sat at her desk feeling puzzled, on the verge of tears, wondering what she'd done wrong and worrying about how she was going to get the meeting set up in time...

Jocelyn's predicament may evoke your compassion. After all, she *was* conscientiously trying to do her job in the best way she knew how. But you might also have some empathy for the actions of her boss, who faced his own pressures and hardly had time to read the essential reports piling up on his desk, much less a long, detailed email about a simple meeting time.

So what was Jocelyn to do?

She could have tried sending the email again and flagging it as an urgent message. Or she might have left her boss a voice mail with the same story.

When I met Jocelyn at one of my seminars, I advised her against both of those options; because I knew she would get the same result. Instead, I gave her a couple of practical techniques for solving the problem. She took my advice and the issue was quickly resolved. Later in this chapter, I'll describe those techniques through simple exercises you can do yourself.

First, however, let's look at some of the reasons Jocelyn wrote the email as she did, and what was behind her boss's response to it.

### *A good hunter must: Stay silent and focused on a single objective*

It may seem a stretch to go back 200,000 years to explain what happened with Jocelyn and Howard. But, as pointed out in the Introduction, the behavior and brains, of both sexes, have been shaped by the actions of our ancient ancestors— the hunters and gatherers of *Homo sapiens* society. To track down a wooly beast for dinner, the males had to wait silently for hours and focus on the one single objective of capturing prey for dinner. The *H. sapiens* female who stayed in the relative safety of the camp, however, had to split her focus in many directions: searching the landscape for berries and keeping one eye on her children, while also leaving her ears open to hear the sounds of a possible violent intruder from another clan or an animal in search of a meal. She and her fellow cavewomen might also keep up a steady stream of noisy chatter to scare off potential animal predators. And the women's voices could rise into a shrill alarm, calling all of the females to join forces together to fight off an attacker, since individually; they did not have the brute strength of the men.

In this setting, the male hunters of ancient times relied heavily on their highly refined visual skills to track and locate the prey— the women depended more on their verbal skills to survive. Besides the evolutionary pressures that emphasized these differences between the sexes, neuroscience now provides evidence that our brains diverge along different gender-based paths as well. Women's brains have many more areas wired for verbal communication, while in men; only a relatively small section in the left hemisphere is devoted to verbal communication. Additionally, while women have numerous active connections between the left and right hemispheres of the brain, men have fewer of those connections. (See more on this subject in the *"Brain Basics"* at the end of this chapter.)

### He doesn't listen! She talks too much!

This biological arrangement is one of the leading causes of frustration, hurt feelings, disagreements and stress between men and women, both in the workplace and at home. "He doesn't listen!" is a common complaint I hear from women, while I get "She talks too much!" from the men.

Let's examine both of those charges.

The idea of females talking "too much" is an accusation that has been leveled at women for centuries, and women have rightfully rejected society's attempts to stifle and silence them. Even today, one of the truisms in popular culture and humor is that women, on a daily basis, use more words than men do. The jury is out on the veracity of this claim, as one study shows that women speak twice the amount of words per day as men, while another claims that both genders use the same amount of words. I tend to subscribe to the second theory. (See details on this issue in the box entitled *"Do women really talk more than men do?"* at the end of this chapter)

Now as to the complaint that men "don't listen," my view is this: It's not so much that men don't listen as it is that men find it harder to process verbal information than women do. Like a pinball machine that's been pushed off balance, men go "tilt" when bombarded with a heavy verbal input. They go on overload. For a woman, her verbal input, especially with a lot of detail, is not only important— it is essential. Because of her highly developed communication skills, a woman needs lots of detail to get the full emotional impact of the communication.

This is not so for a man. Since he cannot process auditory information as easily as can a woman, he relies on his visual skills to interpret the auditory input. The old adage, "a picture is worth a thousand words," is certainly true for him. A man tends to take verbal information and make a picture of it in his mind's eye. If men are assailed with ever-changing details, it becomes difficult, if not impossible, for them to form a clear image of the information. Soon the man becomes overwhelmed, and he begins to shut down in frustration. This frustration may take the form of ignoring you, looking away, cutting you off, deflecting your question by changing the subject, or using other forms of dismissal.

If this happens *to you*, it is important *for you* to understand that the man is not shutting down because of you—personally—

but rather because he is unable to process the information in the way it is being presented. Please also realize that 99 percent of the time he is doing this unconsciously. Even though I know this about myself, I find myself unconsciously "tuning out" when I am hit with a lot of information at once.

Some men, of course, may tune out women by habit, or gruffly cut them off because of unrepentant chauvinistic attitudes. Even in those cases, however, the man may be behaving this way because he's covering up his inability to process the information coming toward him and he doesn't want to appear stupid or weak. Throughout this book, you'll be getting insights and ideas about communicating in different situations that can help you deal with the more difficult members of the male species.

What I want you to understand at this point, is that many men are unaware of how they shut down in the face of too much input from a woman. I can just tell you that, typically, they do—and you need to recognize that reality and adapt to it if you want to be heard.

### Headlines vs. Stories

So let's return to the situation between Jocelyn and Howard. Given that Jocelyn is pre-disposed, in an evolutionary sense, to provide lots of details in her communication, it is not surprising that she wrote her email with all of the particulars about what went into securing the conference room for Howard's meeting. By the same token, Howard's internal wiring caused him to scan the message for its crucial elements, always looking out for any lurking menace that might "kill" him (as a dangerous animal might have literally done to his caveman ancestor on the hunt). Unconsciously, it's as though he's driven to "cut to the chase," which, in a business setting, means getting to the bottom line as fast and as efficiently as possible.

To help Jocelyn be more effective in her job, and to give her some insight into how her boss might have felt about her email, I shared the following conversation I overheard at a family gathering some time ago. My cousin, Mary, was frustrated that her husband, Steve, did not know the details about the birth of a son to his close friend, Bill, and his wife, Ann. The conversation went like this:

*Mary:* "Was it a boy or a girl?"
*Steve:* "It was a boy."
*Mary:* "What's the baby's name? How much did it weigh?"
*Steve:* "I think its name is Jake… John… something like that. He weighed a lot… I don't know."
*Mary:* "How's Ann doing? Is she home from the hospital? I'd like to see her."
*Steve:* "I guess she's doing fine. Bill didn't say otherwise… I don't know if she's home or not… I don't know…"

Have you ever heard—or been involved in—a conversation like that? Have you ever felt like you're "pulling eye teeth" to get a man to give you what you consider to be the important details of a story?

If so, you may have concluded that the guy was clueless—or heartless. But it's not that Steve doesn't care. It is just that, as a male, he's prone to listen for the bottom line.

If this situation were a news story, Steve would only deliver the headline:

"Baby Boy Born: Both Mother and Son Survive."

Mary, by contrast, would report all the details associated with the story:

"… Ann Creagh, 34, of Bloomington delivered a 9-pound, 10-ounce baby boy, named Jonathan Steven Creagh, on Sunday August 24 at Bloomington General Hospital. Both mother and son are doing well and are expected to leave the hospital on Tuesday. This is Mrs. Creagh's third child."

As Steve and Mary demonstrate, men want the headlines—the bottom line first. Women like the story. And both are fine. However, when you are communicating with a man, it's in your interest to make it easy for him to understand and engage with you. Overwhelming him with detail will just frustrate him, resulting in little or no real communication. Most likely, he will be thinking of ways to disengage from talking with you or responding to you.

**Gender Gap Alert:** Since men think and speak in "headlines" most of the time, they tend to believe that anyone who does not do the same is scattered and/or unfocused. Fair or not, you can lose credibility and leverage in a business situation if you do not adjust your communication style to account for this difference between men and women. Remember, men see the world through their filters, not yours.

When Jocelyn heard about the conversation between Steve and Mary, she began to get a better idea of how her email looked to her boss, Howard. With that understanding in mind, Jocelyn and I worked on a few exercises to help make her communications conform to the "headline" model Howard needed. What follows are two exercises that you can apply to your own communication challenges.

**EXERCISE: Five Questions for Quicker Communication**

Before journalists boil their stories down to a headline, they first gather information based on a traditional technique called the "5 W's." You may have heard of that technique, because the fundamental questions every news report must answer are: Who? What? When? Where? And Why? In other words, when you read a story, you want to know: *What* happened, *Who* it happened to, and *When or Where* it happened. You are also usually interested in *Why* it happened, and most good stories try to explain the answers to that question as well.

When Jocelyn looked at what she needed to communicate to Howard through the lens of the "5 W's," she was able to reduce her message to its essence. Here's one draft showing what her email looked like after we worked through this exercise (and you'll see the "5W" questions I added in italics):

Dear Howard,

The Sales Team *(Who)* can be available for the meeting *(What)* with you on Thursday, March 23 at 2 p.m. *(When)* in the West Conference Room *(Where)*, so you can review the new strategic plan with them *(Why)*.

I have already entered the time into the master calendar and will adjust your personal itinerary as soon as you confirm receipt of this message.

Thanks,
Jocelyn

Once Jocelyn got a little more comfortable with this technique, she started honing her messages even more, using bullet points to get across basic information. So if she had to report on simple meeting logistics, she would write something like this:

Dear Howard,
This message is to alert you to:

**Subject:** Sales Staff Meeting
**When:** Thursday, March 23 at 2 p.m.
**Where:** West Conference Room
**Topic:** Review of New Strategic Plan
**Action Required:** Please confirm time so I can adjust the master calendar.

Thanks
Jocelyn

As you can imagine, Howard responded much more positively to these messages than he did to her previous lengthy emails. And Jocelyn reports that their working relationship is much smoother since she changed her approach. "I'm a little embarrassed by the long emails I used to send because I always put in a ton of information," she told me one day after we had worked together. "No one had time to read all of that—especially if they were picking up messages on a cell phone or a BlackBerry®. Now, I 'headline' it and just give the bare-bones information. If they want more detail, then I send the background stuff as an attachment. That way, it's there if they want it."

*Tip:* Besides organizing your emails and other communications around the "5 W" questions, you can also lift another trick from journalists by studying the abbreviated "crawl" summaries that often appear along the bottom of the television screen during a newscast. These short sentence fragments convey the essence of a news story, and are somewhat reminiscent of old-fashioned telegram messages—or new-style text messages. Pay attention to the "crawl" the next time you're watching the news and you may get ideas on how you can make your communications more direct and to the point.

## EXERCISE: Headlines First, Stories Second

The "Five Questions for Quicker Communication" worked well in helping Jocelyn get better responses to her written emails. What about your verbal communications?

As illustrated in the story of Steve telling Mary about the birth of his friend's son, men want headlines first. This exchange between Rhonda, a mid-level manager, and her supervisor, Dan, will show you how you might apply the "headlines-first" rule when speaking to men in your workplace:

To begin, here is Rhonda's conversation when she started with the "story" first instead of the "headline." In this situation, Rhonda wants the permission to fire an employee, Jess, who is continually late for work.

*Rhonda:* Dan, I want to talk with you about Jess. You know he's been with us for more than five years. He came over from our sister division during the merger. I believe he was originally under contract with them at the time. He's been a good employee and worked hard up until last year. I actually gave him a promotion with a good bump in salary. I've liked him, and he seemed to get along well with his coworkers. But now, he's continually late and absent from work. I have talked to him about it, and, you know, he promises that he'll change and he does for a while. But then something seems to come up and he goes back to the same old thing. I feel as though he's taking advantage of my good nature. Some of the others are now complaining because they have to cover for him. I finally had to write him up and he went to HR (Human Resources) in a huff about unfair treatment, age discrimination and all that...I thought that would be the end of it but..."

*Dan* (frustrated): "Rhonda I hate to do this but I need to get ready for a meeting in a few minutes. Why don't we talk later?"

Here is Dan and Rhoda's conversation about this same situation—only this time, Rhonda starts with the "headline" first:

*Rhonda:* "Dan I need to talk with you about Jess. It will take about five minutes. Is this a bad time\*?"
*Dan:* "No this is OK."
*Rhonda:* "In my judgment, the time has come for us to begin the process for terminating Jess for his chronic absenteeism. I want to know your thoughts."
*Dan:* "Hmm...he has been a problem. What have you done so far?"
Rhonda: "I've spoken to him about it numerous times over this past year, and I finally wrote him up. Instead of improving, he complained to HR about me—and he's still coming in late and missing many days of work."

*Dan:* "I agree, then, it's time to start the termination process. Get the paperwork together and let's meet tomorrow to finalize it."

\* *Tip*: Asking if this is a "bad time" is done on purpose. People are so used to hearing, "Is this a *good* time" that they do not really listen to the question. It's similar to when a store clerk asks, "Can I help you?" What is your stock response? Usually, you'll say something like: "No thank you, I'm just looking." What if the clerk instead asked: "Is this your first time in our store?" Now what happens? There's no stock answer on the tip of your tongue, so you must stop, hear the question, and think of a response! The same is true with using the phrase: "Is this a bad time?" It jolts people out of their automatic replies and prods them to actually listen to you.

**Your turn:**

In the space below (or on a separate piece of paper), describe a situation in which you talked to a man and led off the conversation with the "story" first instead of the "headline":

_____

_____

_____

_____

_____

_____

_____

_____

How did the man respond?

_____

_____

_____

_____

_____

_____

Now rewrite it, this time leading with the "headline" first:

_____

_____

_____

_____

_____

_____

*Tip:* If you find yourself getting tangled up in too many words when you're trying to write a report or prepare for a presentation, remember this advice from the television character, Sergeant Joe Friday, who's signature line was: "Just the facts, ma'am." If you're too young to remember Jack Webb playing the part of Sgt. Friday in the 1950s TV series, *Dragnet,* you can watch a DVD of the show (or the movie version of *Dragnet* starring Tom Hanks and Dan Aykroyd), and you will see Sgt. Friday working on criminal cases taken from the files of the Los Angeles Police Department. Whenever a female witness would go on and on with too many superfluous details, Sgt. Friday would politely but firmly re-direct her to stick to the salient points of the story and give him "just the facts, ma'am." When communicating with men, let that phrase guide you and give the guys the "headlines" first—and then more of the details afterwards if they ask for them.

### *Multi-tasking Women in a "One-Thing-at-a-Time" World*

You may now have a clearer picture of how—and why—it is to your benefit to present your messages in bullet-pointed, bite-sized chunks when working with men. And the idea of presenting "headlines" first may also make sense. In other words, you can appreciate the fact that the average man will respond more positively if you send him information in a small-sized package. But what if you have many packages to deliver? What do you do if you have to cover multiple subjects with a male whose ancestral wiring pre-disposes him to stay focused on a single item? How does a typical woman, who's comfortable with multi-tasking, adjust to a "one-thing-at-a-time," male-oriented workplace?

To begin to address those questions, we must once again look at the differences between male and female brains. One way to understand those differences is to look at what the computer world calls "parallel processing" and "serial processing."

### *Parallel vs. Serial Processing*

Women's brains are similar to computers that are capable of parallel processing. Most females can easily handle multiple threads of thought at one time. They can begin with one thought, jump to another and then on to another—keeping track of all of them and moving back and forth among the various ideas if necessary. That's parallel processing.

Men, by contrast, operate like computers that are only capable of serial processing. That is, one task must be completed and saved before a new task can be started. Likewise, the male brain tends to function best when it focuses on one thought or assignment at a time before it moves on to something new. Have you ever opened one program on your computer and received the warning: "Program not responding"? Well, that's exactly what happens when you try to open up too many "programs"—that is, subjects—with a man or to open them up too quickly.

I am not implying that men are incompetent. They are not, nor are women. We each take in and process information in different ways. Understanding this will help you realize what's happening when a man does not seem to be listening or is pushing you away. This is his signal that he is not able to process the information in the way you are delivering it. When this happens, take it as a cue that you need to use a different approach.

### The PAPER Method™

I developed the following technique to help you get the most out of your interactions with men. It is a quite simple five-step process, and I gave it a simple name to make it easy to remember. (Hey, I am a guy, right?)

I call it The PAPER Method™.

**PAPER** is the acronym for these steps:

**P**–PRIORITIZE
**A**–AGREE
**P**–PAUSE
**E**–EXHALE
**R**–REPEAT


Here's how it works:

**EXERCISE: The PAPER Method™**

1. **PRIORITIZE** the topics you want to cover
   a. Ask for input and agreement.
   b. Cover the FIRST topic.

2. **AGREE** on the next steps (who, what, where, when, why, and supporting evidence). Summarize the agreement made at this stage by stating:
   a. *"This is the outcome we want _____ because _____."* (Reasons it is important for both.)
   b. *"I am going to do _____."*
   c. *"You are going to do _____."*
   d. *"These will be done by _____ (date)."*
   e. *"This is how we will measure success/know if it is successful."*
   f. *"If it is not successful then we will _____* (describe next steps, if any)."*

3. **PAUSE and EXHALE** (1—2 seconds)

    a.  Stop for a momentary break to let the other person catch a breath.

    b.  Then ask: *"What do you want to discuss next?"*

**4.  REPEAT** with each topic

## EXAMPLE

(Let's go back to Rhonda, who has three things to discuss with her manager, Dan. They have scheduled 45 minutes for their meeting.)

> Rhonda: *"Hi Dan. We had scheduled 45 minutes for this meeting. Does that still work for you?"**
> Dan: *"Yes."*
> Rhonda: *"So that we get everything accomplished we need to agree to hold any interruptions. Sound fair?"*
> Dan: *"Sure."*
> Rhonda: *"Dan, as I highlighted in my email, I have a few issues that I need to discuss with you today OK?"*
> Dan: *"Sure. What's up?"*

## PRIORITIZE

> Rhonda: *"There are three issues that need your attention:"*

- *The Acme account situation*
- *Overtime for the department*
- *And a potential termination issue with Jess.*

*"Do you have a preference about which one we discuss first?"*

***Dan:*** *"Hmm... Tell me about the Jess issue."*

41

Rhonda gives a straightforward, bare-bones account of the instances of Jess's chronic absenteeism and wants to begin his termination process. Dan agrees. But since Jess has already complained to the Human Resources department, Dan wants to consult with the Legal Department to make sure everything is done according to policy.

## AGREEMENT

Rhonda: *"To sum this up, we both agree that Jess's absenteeism is sending the wrong signals to the rest of the group, and we must begin the termination process. You also indicated that we want to make sure that we are completely clean in how we do this. You will talk to Phil in Legal?"*

Dan: *"Yes."*

Rhonda: *"When do think you can do that and give me a go-ahead?"*

Dan: *"No later than 4 p.m. tomorrow."*

Rhonda: *"Great. Let's talk tomorrow."*

Dan: *"OK."*

Rhonda: *"If you can't get hold of Phil, will you let me know?"*

Dan: *"Yes."*

Rhonda: *"In the meantime, I will draw up the paperwork.*
*Anything else you want to add or change?"*

Dan: *"No. That's it."*

## PAUSE and EXHALE

Taking the time to pause and exhale for one to two seconds is crucial to the success of this technique. This pause, or break in the action, allows the man to metaphorically "save" the information (as a computer would) and then be ready to open up a new "file" for the next item you want to present.

## REPEAT
Go to the next item on your list of three:

> Rhonda: *"That leaves the Acme situation and the question of authorizing department overtime. Which do you want to discuss next?"*
> Dan: *"Acme."*
> Rhonda: *"As you know, we have had problems with them in the past, and…"*

Time and interruption agreements are optional. Use these for people who are not good with time and/or interruptions. This is your time, and you deserve the person's complete attention. You are "teaching" them how they are to treat you. My rule is: If something is likely to happen, such as interruptions, not enough time, typing and/or checking emails, etc., deal with it right away; at the start of the meeting.

There are a few critical elements that make this method work, and you need to take note of them. As already explained, the momentary pause is essential, because it allows the man to "reboot" his internal computer; that is, to digest the information you've given him before opening up to new input. The other important element is to ask the other person to prioritize the order of discussion. The reasons you do this are threefold:

- First, by giving the other person the option of choosing the topic, you create the illusion that he is in control. Actually, *you* are the one in control. You are saying in effect, "*We are going to discuss these topics, and you get to choose the order.*"

- Second, the other person becomes engaged in the discussion; they can't just sit back and listen. They have to choose!
- Lastly, given several options, people will tend to select the ones they are most interested in tackling first. This minimizes the chances of getting bogged down on irrelevant issues.

NOTE: Once you've completed the verbal discussion, be sure to send an email or write a memo briefly confirming details in writing. Having a "paper trail"—or actually, an "email trail"—is an important aspect of being an effective communicator in business today.

**Your Turn:**
Practice **The PAPER Method**™ using a typical situation from your life.

## PRIORITIZE

List the subjects you would like to discuss with a male boss, coworker, spouse, friend, etc. (Obviously, if you have just one subject to discuss, this step is not necessary. However, it is still a good idea to state what that one subject is and ask if he is ready to talk about it.)

1. _____

   _____

2. _____

   _____

3. _____

   _____

Do you have a preference for the one we begin with?

## AGREEMENT

Discuss the issue.

Summarize your understanding of the agreement to this point.

- *Let's see if I have this correct. We agreed to* _____ (agreement) *because* _____ \_\_\_\_\_ (the reason why it is important). *Is that correct? And,*
- *I am going to* _____ _____(your action) *by*_____ (date).
- *You are going to* _____ _____ (their action) *by*_____ (date).
- *We will know this is working, because* _____ (the evidence).
- *If for some reason it doesn't work out, we will* _____ (clearly state what the next step is).
- *Anything else you would like to add:* _____?

## PAUSE and EXHALE

- Allow one to two seconds for him to "save" it mentally and open a new "page" in his thought process.

## REPEAT

- What do you want to discuss next?

Once you've had the chance to put The PAPER Method™ into operation, or to use any of the other exercises from this chapter, you will begin to see a difference in your ability to work with men and get things done. I can make this claim, because so many women who have participated in my seminars tell me that is what has happened for them.

Gena, for instance, reported that her male co-workers and supervisors have become much more relaxed and cooperative with her since she started applying these communication techniques. "I used to hit them with a list of 15 things that had to get done," she says. "Now I just go in with three items (or four at the most) and I bottom line everything. When I tried The PAPER Method™ with my boss, I could see this smile come across his face and it was like he was saying, 'You're communicating with me for the first time.'"

In fact, Gena was so excited about her positive results at work, she decided to try The PAPER Method™ on her husband to discuss their upcoming vacation plans. "I told him I had three things to talk with him about," she says. "And then I asked what he wanted to talk about first. He was kind of blown away. I could see him switching on a gear that he's never shown me before in all our years of marriage. It was phenomenal."

Remember: You *can* get your messages across, and you *can* be heard, if you are willing to adjust your communication style so the men in your life have a chance to address one thing at a time.

## BRAIN BASICS

### White Matter—Gray Matter

The brain is composed of two types of tissue—gray matter and white matter. Men have approximately 6.5 times the amount of gray matter compared to that of women related to general intelligence; but women have nearly ten times the amount of white matter—according to a study spearheaded by psychology professor Richard Haier of the University of California, Irvine. "These findings suggest that human evolution has created two different types of brains designed for equally intelligent behavior," Haier has said, in regard to the study's results. Neuropsychologist Rex Jung of the University of New Mexico, who co-authored the study, said that its results might help explain why men and women excel at different types of tasks. One possibility suggested by this research is that women are better at integrating and assimilating information from distributed gray-matter regions of the brain—which may explain the female propensity for multi-tasking (or "parallel processing," in computer jargon.) Men, Jung reported, tend to do better with tasks requiring more localized processing—and that may account for the type of thinking characterized as "serial processing" in the computer world. The study, entitled *"The neuroanatomy of general intelligence: sex matters"* appeared in the online version of the journal, *NeuroImage* (1/16/05).

### Do Women Really Talk More Than Do Men?

There is more than a little controversy in academic circles about whether women talk more than men do. I have seen statistics supporting the idea that women say approximately

20,000 words per day, on average, while men speak about 7,000. Other sources postulate that women talk twice as much as men. I am not certain that is the case. I know many men who talk a great deal and women who are quiet. I believe the main difference is that men tend to be silent when they are thinking or figuring something out, whereas women prefer to talk through a vexing problem. In my experience, both genders seem to speak about the same amount. A study reported in *Science* magazine (July 6, 2007, issue) seems to confirm my suspicions. The study, (led by researcher Matthias Mehl at the University of Arizona) found that men and women talk about the same amount—approximately 16,000 words (electronically activated recorder) for several days. Sometimes, it seems, our perceptions about the opposite sex are really misperceptions that can get in the way of our working effectively together.

## Are You Working Harder Than You Need To?

The female tendency for including numerous descriptive details in written and verbal communication can serve women well in some situations. Being interested in and able to keep track of all the personal and "political" nuances affecting a business negotiation, for instance, can be an advantage. But when women put too much information into their communication of email, voice mail or presentations to men in a business setting, their work almost literally "falls on deaf ears." Males, typically, become overloaded when faced with excess input. That holds true, also, when women write up information for performance reviews or MBO (Management by Objective) reports.

As Lynn, a long-time Executive Assistant, told me: "Women give all sorts of background and detail in their MBOs, while the men will only put in two or three bullet points. It seems as though the women always make it harder on themselves than the men do because they only write one sentence for each point and don't give any details. Maybe the women are overachievers, and the men don't want to put too much in, because they might be held accountable... I don't know... But, to me, it looks like the women make themselves work harder, and I'm not sure they have to." Another explanation is that for women, with their emphasis on people and relationships, offering lots of detail is important. It demonstrates that they have really put a great deal of thought into the performance review or the other person. Men, by contrast, with their focus on things, (that is, the "bottom line") see no need to add a lot of detail: "Marilyn is doing a great job." End of story.

I believe there is another dynamic also at play behind the male's penchant for succinctness: protection. We know that in our world of never-ending competition, the more information we give, the more chances the information can be used as "ammunition" against us by other males.

Women, it seems, give you the details and let you intuit the bottom line, while men give you the bottom line and let you intuit the details.

**Talking in Technicolor**
"Women talk in Technicolor and men talk in black and white!" my consultant friend Fran shared. "Women give all the details and men want the bottom line," listen to the details afterward. Otherwise, they'll be listening to you and

thinking 'Where is this going? What do you want?' They won't necessarily say anything to you about it, either. It depends on the relationship. In some cases, the men will just lose interest, or get impatient or just go into their heads and start thinking about something else. Or, if the guy is your boss, he may ask you 'Where are you going with this?' Even though I'm aware of this difference between men and women, I don't always talk 'bottom line.' And when I don't, I watch the eyes of the men glaze over. That's when I try to catch myself and start being more succinct."

## Chapter 3: Know Your Place in the Pack

"I felt like I was in a room with a bunch of little kids," Gail said, in exasperation during our coaching session to discuss her problems with a recent staff meeting. "One guy started bragging about how much better *his* department was doing than anyone else's. Another guy jumped in to tell everyone about how much money *he* saved the company when he ran that department…"

Gail went on to say, "Soon, every man in the room got in on the act, bragging about their own achievements and talking so fast she could hardly take notes."

"And to top it off," Gail added, "none of it had anything to do with the actual topic of the meeting, except that they had done something better than someone else at some point in their lives. I finally gave up."

Gail's description of that meeting perfectly mirrors the frustration many women experience when they deal with one of the most common features of male communication: one-upmanship.

I'm sure you're familiar with the concept, but for the record, "one-upmanship" occurs when one man shows up another man by having greater results, honors, knowledge, expertise, possessions or personal connections. That puts him in a position to be one step higher—or "one-up"—over his competitor.

As did Gail, many women dismiss this search for status as a silly, childish game. But to males, it is anything but silly.

A man needs to know—down to the core of his being—where he stands in relation to another man and what is his position among a group of men. They have to know their place in the pack. This need is not just an abstract intellectual exercise; it is essential to their very identities as males.

This jockeying for position happens everywhere for men—and *all* the time—whether they work as cab drivers or CEOs, salesmen or brain surgeons. Men will compete over anything, regardless of whether it's an important business issue, like posting the highest sales results, or something less crucial, such as having the coolest tie. Even a domestic chore, like mowing the lawn, can get the competitive juices flowing for men. As shown in the 2008 movie, *Rachel Getting Married*—men will even compete over who can load a dishwasher the fastest!

The virtual world is offering a new arena for male one-upmanship as well. One of the women in my communication seminar told me this story that was making the rounds in her office: When setting up a video conference call with a division head in another part of the country, one vice president went out of his way to display an expensive piece of original art in his office. Sure enough, when the next video call was set up in the office of the division head, he had an even *more* expensive art piece as a backdrop behind him.

That's one-upping.

This behavior is ingrained in our DNA. Just as searching for the bottom line (discussed in Chapter 2) is an unconscious default mechanism for men, so too is the quest for status. Men have done it their whole lives. It's automatic.

And it's not all bad.

Competition has obviously led to countless discoveries throughout history—and many of the advances in science and technology that we take for granted might never have happened were it not for healthy competition, among men *and* women.

But what drives this competition?

## A Good Hunter: Must be Able to Fight to be the Best

If you recall from our discussion in the Introduction, modern males often echo the behavior of their cavemen ancestors, and one of the hallmarks of a *Homo sapiens* hunter was that he had to fight to be the best. Doing anything less than that might result in his being killed by a dangerous animal.

Besides his obvious benefit of staying alive, the more successful the hunter, the more power—and rewards—he received: first pick of the females, largest share of the food, warmest spot in the cave and so on.

The top male hunter also got respect and deference from his male peers, because his skills proved that he was vital to the survival of the group. Unlike most of our post-modern world, threats to survival were real and immediate. Survival, then, was paramount, and each man vigorously competed to be the best, or the "alpha male," because that gave him a chance to pass on his genes to future generations. (For more on this idea, and other terms that describe male hierarchies (See *"Top Dogs and Alpha Males."* And *"Brain Basics"* at the end of the chapter for further insights).

On the flip side of the coin, if a man was not near the front of the pack, he was far less likely to get the rewards of food and females. The loss of status and/or power in the group equaled "emotional death" to those of lower status. Ultimately, it meant their DNA died out too, since they had fewer chances to pass on their genes.

The prime motivator for the *H. sapiens* hunter, then, was the acquisition of power and status through his accomplishments.

Getting and keeping power is still a constant struggle for men—and the source of the "one-upmanship" you see at work (and probably at home as well). It also fuels the turf battles, the sniping over titles, and the competition over salary levels and job rankings within corporations and other businesses (See *"Are You on the Level?" at the end of this chapter*).

The struggle for power can also be observed in a typical business meeting. The men enter and quickly scan the room for "their" chair. The chair they pick indicates where they believe they fit within the hierarchy. The men instinctively know that the head of the table is usually reserved for the alpha male. Those on either side are the next in rank and so on. Sometimes a lower-ranked male will attempt to increase his status by taking the chair of one of the more senior members. This is part of the jousting for status that colors everything men do. Again, a great deal of this positioning occurs at the subconscious level.

At the beginning of a meeting, the males will often be talking about a winning sports team, their recent golf game or a deal they just closed. They will tease each other by "innocently" pointing out another's faux pas. To the casual listener, this banter seems like "boys being boys," and it is. However, these conversations are, as my mother used to say, "half-fun and full-earnest," meaning putdowns disguised as jest. These jabs are a way for men to both bond and gain status within the group. They get "one-up" in status by putting another "one down." For the most part, the "one-down" person does not get upset, because he knows his turn will come to return the favor (and we'll look more closely at this aspect of male behavior in Chapter 3). For women, all of this one-upmanship seems absurd. Female bonding requires empathy, sharing and maintaining the relationship. You don't bond by putting someone down. By contrast, for men, arguing, fighting and putdowns are all part of connecting to each other and they consider it "business as usual."

### Get in Line and Get to Work

Given the pervasiveness of male one-upmanship, you may wonder how any work gets done. But if you look at that typical business meeting a little more closely, you will observe an interesting phenomenon. As soon as the alpha male takes his place at the head of the table, the boyish banter virtually stops. The men rivet their attention on the leader and start focusing on the business at hand. (Incidentally, if a woman is in the "alpha male" position, the men will tend to behave the same way. See more on this in *"Your Place in the Pack"* at the end of this chapter).

In some sense, when the alpha male takes his place, it's as though the men can "relax," because the hierarchy is now established. Each man knows where he stands and what's expected of him. It's not as though he can let down his guard entirely—that's a rare luxury. But once the "top dog" or alpha male brings order to the unruly pack, the individual men can temporarily suspend their one-upmanship and give their allegiance to the leader. Like a platoon of soldiers called to attention, or a football team responding to the quarterback's signals, the men get in line and get to work.

That's exactly what happened at the meeting Gail attended where she threw up her hands in exasperation over the antics of her bragging male co-workers.

As Gail tells it: "Once my boss sat down and started paying attention, I noticed the other men started paying attention too! I realized that they mirror him, and if he's taking a speaker seriously, then they also start taking that person seriously."

That insight, and our coaching sessions, took a great deal of stress out of her job, Gail reported. She was able to streamline her note taking and recognize priorities more easily.

"When I was a new team member," Gail explains, "I had difficulty figuring out what was going on. I couldn't tell whether something was an action item, or something they already knew, or something that was just a matter of 'one-upping' each other."

"Finally" she adds, "I realized I didn't have to write down every single word. Now I just wait until the 'one-upping' is over and then I start taking notes. That's been a *big* timesaver for me."

*Tip:* Besides opening her ears to distinguish between banter and serious talk, Gail also trained her eyes to notice the body language of her male co-workers. Like Gail, you too can pay attention to the facial expressions and postures of the men you work with. If a guy is typing on his laptop and smirking, it's a good bet he's "one-upping" another guy—not compiling a quarter-end report. Or, watch how men who've been leaning back in their chairs suddenly sit up straight once the "alpha male" calls a meeting to order. By becoming aware of these behaviors, you will be better able to pick the opportune moments to deliver your own communications—and make sure you're not ignored when the men are simply jostling each other for position and not really paying attention.

**EXERCISE: Can You Spot Who's On Top?**
Instead of dismissing, ignoring or attempting to override sessions of male one-upmanship, instead, try observing this behavior objectively. Remember, at least for the time being, you're the anthropologist studying foreigners. Use this exercise to step back and take a broader view of male culture.

**Your turn:**

In the space below (or on a separate piece of paper), write your answers to these questions:

*Can you remember an incident or situation at work where men were "one-upping" each other? What happened?*

_____

_____

_____

_____

_____

_____

_____

_____

*What did each man say or do?*

_____

_____

_____

_____

_____

_____

*How was it resolved?*

_____

_____

_____

_____

_____

_____

*Once it was over, what did you think of the incident?*

_____

_____

_____

_____

_____

_____

*Have you changed your mind about the incident now that you know more about how men use "one-upping" to establish order amongst themselves?*

_____

_____

_____

_____

_____

_____

This one simple exercise is not necessarily going to make it any easier for you to enjoy sitting around with a bunch of guys while they're trying to top each other. But you can use it when you need to sort out workplace behavior that may otherwise baffle you. Also, as you go about your day-to-day activities, pay attention to men's conversations and see if you can begin to hear the one-up/one-down theme in their conversations. You will be amazed and fascinated by it. Notice too, how much men enjoy this banter. You will start to understand how wonderfully different men are from women!

## Bragging Rights

Now let's move on to another aspect of the struggle for status that has a special importance in the workplace. Women need to realize that whether "one-upping" is subtle or obnoxious, it gives males rights that females generally do not enjoy: bragging rights.

From the successful *H. sapiens* hunter to the exuberant football fan to the negotiator who steals an account from a competitor, men naturally celebrate their triumphs through braggadocio.

An experience I had early in my career brought this lesson home to me. I was doing a sales training for Sharon's company. For some reason, the sales area had been set up with a men's section and a women's section. Sharon wasn't sure how this arrangement came about, but it was great for seeing gender differences firsthand.

While everyone in the sales department was required to make calls, set appointments and, ultimately, close the sale, the women were going about their jobs without much fanfare. The men, on the other hand, were quite different. When one of them got an appointment or landed a sale, he stood up and yelled across the cubicles about his accomplishment. That crowing led to mild heckling from his cohorts: "Even a blind squirrel finds a nut sometime." or "Who closed it for you?"

Both the boasting and the good-natured put downs are expected from men to men by men. Telling the others about snagging the client was a way for the salesman to go "one-up" on the others, while the retorts gave the hecklers a chance to reclaim their status.

As noted earlier, this behavior is so ingrained that it's below the level of consciousness. In fact, when I asked some of the salesmen if they realized their heckling could be seen as put-downs, virtually all of them responded by saying "I was just teasing him!" Only after reflection did some of them admit that they felt a little better after having made the remark. That's understandable, because it restored a sense of balance to the individual and to the group.

For women, it's hard to comprehend how the boasting, and the accompanying put-downs, can give men the opportunity to bond and grow closer, while it simultaneously puts them down or in their place in order to maintain the hierarchy.

Like the woman at Sharon's company, most females tend to shy away from boasting or bragging because it is considered rude and out of place. The unwritten rule in female culture is that everyone has a voice and the idea of building up your status by putting someone else down is not done (at least not to the other woman's face).

But if women don't brag, how are they going to let their bosses and colleagues know about their accomplishments while staying true to their female selves?

The simple answer is: Just do it.

I remember feeling uncomfortable making a formal bow and presenting my business card with both hands to a client in Japan. I was uncomfortable only because it was something unfamiliar and unpracticed. However, I knew that this ritual was considered the proper form of introduction in my client's culture, and I wanted to acknowledge that fact and be appropriate.

Did I give up anything by following the ritual? Obviously not. In fact I actually gained. I gained my client's respect, which opened the door for building rapport. Over time, as the rapport and trust grew, the differences between our two cultures became less apparent with each of us adopting the other's customs. We did that to such an extent, that in subsequent meetings, our behavior became a mixture of customs from both our cultures.

The same can and will happen as women enter into men's groups and vice versa. When you are participating with a predominately male group, notice their rituals. How do the men let the others know that they are competent or skilled, and, most importantly, that they can help the group win?

It's likely that I did not make the perfect bow to my Japanese client. But I made the effort and did it in a way that was authentic. By the same token, you, as a woman, do not have to jump up and down and brag like your male counterparts, nor get entangled in their "one-upmanship" games. You just need to come close and behave in a way that rings most true for you.

By now you must be asking yourself: "How do I pull this off?" Perhaps the following interchanges will be helpful in answering that question.

**EXAMPLE:**

Jane has just joined a new company as a software engineer. She is attending a meeting with several other lead engineers (Bill, Steve and Tim) to discuss the launch of a new project. All participants are male except Jane. John, the Program Manager, begins the meeting:

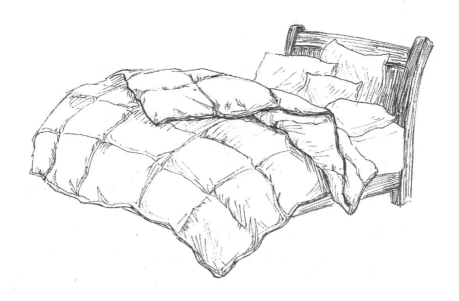

*John:* "As you know, this is a very important program for the company, and we must get it right and on time. There will be no room for mistakes."

*Bill:* "So what's new?" (Laughter)

*Steve:* "Time to break out the cots and coffee for the 24/7 work week!" (Groans)

*Tim:* "Aw... man-up. You all sound like little girls. Oops... sorry Jane!"

*Jane:* "No problem. I was wondering, though: Do the cots come with comforters?" (Laughter)

*Jane:* "Seriously, though, I know the project sounds tough, but it really seems like an exciting challenge!"

Jane has accomplished two things in this exchange. First, she diffused a potentially uncomfortable situation in which the men could feel they have to walk on eggshells around her. She avoided getting caught up in the one-up/one-down ritual by injecting some humor into the situation. Secondly, she signaled that although she is female, she is also part of the team. She did not require special treatment and was not afraid of a challenge. Notice how Jane also deftly skirted Tim's attempt to enhance his status by the one down statement:"Aw... man-up."

Read on to find out what happened next.

*Tim:* "Jane's right. We've been there and done that before. It has been a lot of work and also a lot of fun."

*John:* "Since this is a large complex project, I've broken it down into the several bite-sized pieces: 101, 102, 103, 104 and 105. I'll assign team leaders for each piece who will then assemble their teams. Then we'll set a timeline and meet once a week as a group to go over the progress. Any questions?"

*Bill:* When are you going to assign the group leaders?

*John:* I'm coming to that. Before I make the assignments, does anyone have a preference? (Silence)

*Jane:* "In my last job, I was on a team that worked on 102, so I am very familiar with the ins and outs of it, and I know how to deal with anything tricky.

*John:* "Thanks, Jane. Any others?"

*Bill:* "Like Jane, I have experience with one of these pieces, number 104, so that would be the logical piece for me."

*Steve:* "I'll take 103. That leaves 101 for Tim. Maybe he'll change his mind on the cot!"

*John:* "Unless anyone has questions, please put your teams together and a project development timeline. We'll meet next Thursday to go over them. Anything else?" (Silence)

*John:* "Good. See you next Thursday at 10 a.m."

Building on her positioning from the beginning of this exchange, Jane continued to show that she considers the project to be an exciting challenge and not a problem. She's showing her "can-do" attitude. She also raised her status within the group by speaking up and simply stating the fact that she had experience with "102" and could make the best contribution there. The others followed with their qualifications. At an unconscious level, Jane is certainly seen as a member of the group, if not the alpha. She was the first to speak up. Finally notice how Steve sought to restore his status by poking a jab at Tim.

If Jane were more comfortable taking part in the one-up/one down game, the interaction would take on a different tone. Like this:

*John:* "As you know, this is a very important program for the company, and we must get it right and on time. There will be no room for mistakes."

*Bill:* "So what's new? "(Laughter)

*Steve:* "Time to break out the cots and coffee for the 24/7 workweek!" (Groans)

*Jane:* "I thought you were men, not a bunch of little boys needing naptime! (Said in a playful tone)

*Tim:* "Listen to her! There will be no time off for hair appointments!"

*Jane:* "Or video games! Really, though, this seems like a great challenge."

*Bill:* "Yeah it could be a lot of fun."

*Tim:* "Jane's right. We've been there and done that before. It has been a lot of work and also a lot of fun."

*John:* "Since this is a large complex project, I've broken it down into the several bite size pieces: 101, 102, 103, 104 and 105. I'll assign team leaders for each piece who will then assemble their teams. Then we'll set a timeline and meet once a week as a group to go over the progress...any questions?"

*Bill:* When are you going to assign the group leaders?

*John:* I'm coming to that. Before I make the assignments, does anyone have a preference? (Silence)

*Jane:* "In my last job I was on a team that worked on 102, so I am very familiar with the ins and outs of it, and, I know how to deal with anything tricky."

*John:* "Thanks Jane. Any others?"

*Bill:* "Like Jane, I have experience with one of these pieces, number 104, so that would be the logical piece for me."
*Steve:* "I'll take 103."
*Tim:* "That leaves 101 for me, which is great."
*John:* "Wow! This came together easier than I had expected. Thanks everyone."
*Jane:* "Maybe there *will* be time for naps."
*Steve:* "And an occasional hair appointment."
*Jane:* "Now you're talking!"

As you can see, in this case Jane got right in there with the men playing the one-up/one-down game. Because she was comfortable with this tactic of joining in with the group, she was able to deliver the jab in a playful way that came across as authentic. Most importantly, she spoke up about her own accomplishments and delivered the message that she is a competent engineer, a team player and a leader.

Jane's story is but one example of how to navigate through the male minefield at work. You will have to experiment to find what works for you. If you want to be heard, and if you want to succeed, you have to be able to authentically toot your own horn and let others know what you've done.

As a man, it's very surprising to me how difficult this can be for women. I've seen tears streaming down the faces of women in my seminars when we broach the subject of their achievements. I'm amazed that so many women—regardless of where they rank in the corporate world—struggle with this issue. (We'll touch on this subject elsewhere in the book, particularly with the "Exceptional You" exercise in Chapter 4.)

Not all women, of course, are shrinking violets when it comes to letting other people know what they've done. Vivian, a high-powered vice-president, has no trouble alerting others to her accomplishments. But she does it in her own way, without sounding like a desperate male trying to move up the ladder. When I asked her about that, here's what she told me: "In a healthy-ego manner, women have to weave their success stories into their communications. It's very important that women do this— if they aren't speaking about their successes, no one else will be. Just drop something about your experience and achievements into the conversation. Don't wait to be asked!"

*Remember, in men's eyes, if you are not flaunting your abilities, they assume you don't have any!* After all, that's how they do it in their world. Men don't see bragging or boasting as bad: It's part of their "cultural norms," and it's what's expected by other males. In fact, they don't give it a first or second thought. It's just as natural as breathing!

Once you get some practice in speaking up about your capabilities, it will be natural to you too. And when you develop your own confident style of communication, you won't have to worry about who's up or down—because you'll be in the strongest position of all.

## Top Dogs and Alpha Males

Did you ever wonder where these labels for men come from? While no one can be completely certain about word origins, here is one theory about how the title of "top dog" emerged. Long ago, when large planks of wood had to be cut by hand, the timber was laid over a pit. Then one man managed the top handle of a two-handed saw, while another man took the bottom handle in the pit below. Because the irons used to hold the wood in place were called "dogs," the man above the pit eventually earned the name "top dog." Meanwhile, the man in the pit who was on the receiving end of the sawdust and wood chips would be the obvious "bottom dog" or "underdog." As for "alpha males," it seems to have originated in studies of animals, particularly wolf packs. In biological terms, it usually refers to the "reproductive success" of the alpha animal, success that is ensured or enhanced by his dominance over the other males in the pack and his access to the healthiest females.

## Brain (See Appendix)

**Amygdala:** Located in the anterior of the temporal lobe, the "amygdala" is almond-shaped and derives from the Greek term "amydale" (almonds). The amygdala is larger and more active in men than it is in women. Because this neural structure triggers aggression, it is the source of male competitiveness and one of the reasons men engage in more overt one-up/one-down behavior than do women. It is also thought to be the contributing factor that causes some males to rapidly transform from a calm state to a fighting one.

## Are You on the Level?

Connie could never understand why her husband constantly talked about his job classification level at work. "He was really touchy about it," she recalls. "He was always worried about how many levels down he was from a particular position or how many levels up. And he'd take time telling me the details, like: 'This is how far down I am now,' or 'This is what the reorganization did to me.' " To Connie, her husband's focus on his job status made no sense, particularly if his salary had not changed. "I'd ask him about it," she says, "and he'd just respond with 'I went down four levels!' like that was supposed to mean something to me. I'd point out to him that he was in the same group with the same team and making close to the same salary, so I couldn't understand what the problem was." After participating in my communication seminar and learning about the importance of one-up/one-down rituals among men, Connie began to have more appreciation for her husband's struggle with the hierarchy at work. "Now," she says, "I listen more attentively and ask more questions. If he says, 'I got bumped up two levels,' I cheer him on and say 'That's great!' Or if he tells me that a vice president sat in on his presentation, I congratulate him, because I know that means a rise in his status. I take the time and share in his excitement. Whereas before, I would have dismissed it all as no big deal."

## Your Place in the Pack

When the hierarchy has been established among a group of men, they instinctively "snap to" and get down to work together, because they have a clear leader and they understand what's expected of them. If someone starts to get out of line, the others may light-heartedly (or roughly) put him back in his place to maintain the order and equilibrium of the group—and to maintain their own status. But what happens when a woman enters the mix? Where are the guys supposed to place her? This can throw them off, and they may respond in any number of ways that a woman would see as being inappropriate. They might ignore, challenge or belittle her—partially, as a test to see where she "fits" in the overall scheme of things.

Curiously (at least to women), if men perceive the woman to be a leader, they will follow her. You see: *Most men in business are not as concerned with whether the leader is a male or a female, as long as that person can help them win.* Men, generally, will follow anyone the group thinks has the best chance of leading the team to victory. Think of the women leaders in history and our current day: Joan of Arc, Margaret Thatcher, Indira Gandhi, Golda Meier, and Eleanor Roosevelt, as well as Hillary Clinton and Meg Whitman (former CEO of eBay). Through their actions, these women showed that they could help their "team" (whether a nation or a company) win.

On the opposite end of the spectrum, if another man is perceived as weak, the others know he is less likely to help the group survive and win— they shun or avoid him. When a female enters a male-dominated work group, she has to show that she fits within the hierarchy, either as the leader or as a competent contributor. Otherwise, the men will treat her just as poorly as they would treat other low-ranking males— which, in turn, makes the women feel disrespected. That is why it is crucial for women to get over their discomfort about highlighting their accomplishments and to speak up in an honest way about their capabilities. You have to show them you're a winner. Remember: To men, if you are not flaunting your abilities, they assume you don't have any!

**Tip:** You have heard that "laughter is the best medicine," and it is. Adding appropriate humor to your interactions with others reduces tension and increases rapport. Done right, it can make the difference between success and failure.

## Chapter 4: "I Win. You Lose. Next Game!" ™

Two men punch each other repeatedly, until finally, a winner emerges and lifts his arms in victory while the loser sprawls on the floor, completely defeated.

And what do these battered and bloodied men do once their fight is finished?

They shake hands!

That's how a clean boxing match ends.

Even if you're not a fan of the sport, you can still marvel at the sight of that handshake between the winner and the loser of a prizefight. Because here you have two people who've been trying to beat each other senseless—and yet *when it's over, it's over.*

In the business arena, the fights don't get as physically rough as they do in the boxing ring (well, not usually, anyway). Yet males in the workplace follow the same code of conduct as professional boxers. After a grueling argument or a screaming match, the men seem able to shrug off the conflict and socialize with each other over drinks or dinner. Perhaps they don't make a beer run immediately after an intense confrontation. But usually, men are able to bounce back from business spats much more quickly than women—some of whom never forget a fight once it takes place.

Why is that? Why do men seem able to engage in these hostile actions and yet still do business together?

To explain this behavior to the women at my seminars, I came up with a phrase that encapsulates one of the central mottoes that rules the lives of men: "I win. You lose. Next game!"™"

In the never-ending struggle for status that always simmers below the surface of male consciousness, every endeavor is seen as a competition where someone wins and someone loses. As explained in Chapter 3, men need to know where they stand in relation to other men and within the male hierarchy. No one hands them their place in the pack, they have to fight for it.

Once the battle ends and a winner is declared, however, the matter is dropped. The winner gains status—at least for the moment and the loser lets it go—at least for the moment. Both men know they will "live to fight another day." The victor in one situation may well be the defeated party in another. That's where the "Next game!" part of the motto comes in—there's always another battle to fight. The winner knows he has to stay on his toes to retain his higher status and the loser looks for an opportunity to move up by trying again—by winning the "Next game!" Generally, in everyday business dealings, these power struggles don't become grudge matches, because the men know there's always a "next time." After all, your enemy today may be your teammate tomorrow.

To women, who put a high value on cooperation in the workplace, the whole idea of the zero-sum game of "I win. You lose." is stressful and counterproductive. Female business culture tends to run on relationships and a continuous stream of connections. Women are more likely to subscribe to the motto "Together We Win!" rather than the win-lose code of the men. Having confrontations creates the risk that relationships could be severed, which is why many women avoid them. It's a rare woman who is comfortable with the idea of having a shouting match with someone and then going out to dinner together.

Now I know you may be thinking that there are plenty of women who can scream with the best of them, and there are some men who nurse wounds and don't "get over it" or move on to the next game when they've been bruised in a business battle (See *"When men—or women—don't move on to the next game" at the end of this chapter*). Nevertheless, I contend that men know—and grow up knowing—that they play on a field designed to create winners and losers. It's hardwired in their DNA! And women do themselves no favors if they try to ignore this win-lose dynamic or pretend it does not exist.

Which tangled threads of the past—and the synapses—brought us to this current state of affairs? In the next section, we'll look at the primal roots of the male credo, "I win. You lose. Next game!™"

### A Good Hunter: Must be Able to Forget the Fight

When tracing our primal roots back to our cave-dwelling ancestors, we see that competition to be the best hunter led to important rewards—more access to food and females—for the *Homo sapiens* male. While that competition was fierce, it was seldom deadly. In a small band of hunters and gatherers in *H. sapiens* society, everyone who could contribute to the food supply was precious. The group could not afford to have a member killed or injured unnecessarily. Life was simply too brutal and harsh.

Even though the men could be very aggressive with each other when vying for power and dominance, they did not usually kill one another. They threatened, made mock attacks, yelled and no doubt pushed each other around. However, that was usually the end of it. After an altercation produced a clear winner and loser, peace was restored, and, most importantly for our discussion, the fight was forgotten.

Watch any nature documentary, and you will find countless examples of two males threatening an attack, screeching at each other or even butting heads to establish dominance. In the end, however, one animal is victorious and the other moves on, (as many species do not engage in death matches with their own kind). You will also see the loser participating in group activities (for example, hunting) as if nothing had ever happened. In other words, the battle is over, balance has returned to the group, and that's that.

In human society, that same behavior pattern for survival is ingrained into our DNA—which explains, in part, how males developed the win-lose paradigm that governs their lives.

### *The Elephant That Never Forgets... and the Man with Nothing on His Mind*

Besides the ancestral legacy of the hunter-gatherer society, another important factor influences the male's ability to forget a fight once it's over: the hippocampus.

The hippocampus is the area of the brain where memories are formed. Actually, it's considered the brain's center for memory—and emotion. This area of the brain has a significant impact on your work and personal relationships because of this fact: the hippocampus is larger and more active in women than in men. No wonder then, women can often recall not only the details of their first date with a new boyfriend, but also everything they said during every argument before they break up. Some researchers even refer to the hippocampus as "the elephant that never forgets" (Read more about this in the section on *"Brain Basics at the end of this chapter"*).

The very structure of our brains, then, makes men more adept than women at relegating the past to the past. Perhaps now you won't be so confused when you see two male colleagues laughing and joking together when only hours before they might have seemed ready to kill each other.

While we're on the subject of the memory and mental processing, you might want to recall this fact from Chapter 2; women have more connective tissue (white matter) in the brain, while men have more processing tissue (grey matter). All of those brain connections tend to make women better assimilators than men. By contrast, men are often more adept at compartmentalization and focusing narrowly on decision-making.

One metaphor that I've found useful in understanding these male-female differences is to imagine men's brains as being filled with little tiny containers. Each container is dedicated to one and only one subject. There is a container for food, one for sex, another for sports, another for business and... you get the point. When a man wants to think about a particular business issue, his brain goes to that container, opens it and brings it into his awareness.

Another thing about these containers in men's brains: They do not touch each other. Each one is completely separate from all the others. The containers can only be opened one at a time. Before the man can move to a different task or subject, the current container must be closed and stored away before a new one can be opened as we saw in Chapter 2. For men, having two containers open at the same time is difficult if not impossible. This ability to compartmentalize is one of the reasons men resist mixing business and personal issues. It may also help explain why famous politicians and preachers can get involved in sexual escapades that end their careers—they simply wall off their public and professional lives, and put them into a separate brain compartment from their libidos.

Men also have one container that drives women crazy. It's the "empty" container. The one called: "Nothing!" How many times have you asked the man in your life: "What are you thinking about?" To which he responds: "Nothing!" I am here to tell you *that is an accurate statement!* Oh there may be some fleeting fragments of thought. But nothing that rises to the level of a real thought. Real thoughts require the man to open a specific container. By the way, men love the "empty" container and will open it often *in order to recharge.* A male boss or significant other may bark at you for interrupting him when he seems to be doing nothing; but in fact, he's actually re-energizing his mental batteries by going to the "empty" container in his brain.

Women, on the other hand, do not have individual containers. In fact they don't have containers at all. Women's brains can be thought of as being a mass of circuits where everything is connected to everything else. They certainly don't have a container called "empty." They don't even have an OFF/ON switch. They have an ALWAYS-ON switch! If you take a look at photos of brain scans showing male and female brains "at rest," you'll see what I'm talking about. The males may have some illumination in a few discrete areas, but the female brains are lit up like Christmas trees—even when they are supposedly "relaxing."

I wanted to take this time to go over some of these fundamental differences in the male and female brain to help you appreciate the problems that can arise if you cling to the idea that men and women think alike. Clearly they don't.

And men and women also don't think in the same way about one of the key truths of male business culture: IT'S NOT PERSONAL.

To men, with their hunter heritage and compartmentalizing brains, business is business and it's not personal. The men recognize that their arguments and one-upmanship moves (see Chapter 3) are all part of the unceasing contest called "I Win. You Lose. Next Game!™"

I'm not saying that men like this situation or that they always handle it gracefully. But if a male CEO has to fire a male vice president who's been a long-time employee, he'll do it—and both men will ultimately acknowledge the decision as the "price of business," not a personal affront. If a man is trying to move up from middle management and a colleague out-maneuvers him for a promotion, he recognizes it's not personal—it's business—and he gets back in the game. Women are certainly capable of similar impersonal behaviors, but it's not ingrained in their gender's cultural expectations in the same way as it is for men.

### It's Not Personal

Because they are immersed in male business culture, men usually nod their heads in agreement when I start talking about this idea and say that business behavior is not personal.

Women, however, often have a different reaction. Margaret, a veteran executive who's come through several Silicon Valley mergers, strongly disagreed with my point of view one day over coffee. "You can say it's nothing personal," she protested, "but it really damn well IS personal."

This divide between male and female perception is vividly illustrated in two movies that are the polar opposites from each other: the classic violent movie about the mafia, *The Godfather*, and the 1998 romantic comedy, *You've Got Mail*, which starred Tom Hanks and Meg Ryan.

One of the most quoted lines from *The Godfather* is taken from the scene where Michael Corleone says to his brother, "It's not personal, Sonny. It's strictly business."

In *You've Got Mail*, Tom Hanks tries that line on Meg Ryan to explain what happened after his large chain bookstore put her small independent shop out of business. When Hanks says, "It wasn't personal," Ryan shoots back with: "…What is *that* supposed to mean? I am so sick of that. All it means is it's not personal to *you*, but it's personal to *me*, it's personal to a lot of people. What's wrong with personal, anyway?"

So there it is: A man on one side claiming that a business deal is "not personal," and a woman on the other, insisting that it is.

A typical male might say the man is right and that women just need to get over it. But as I've stated earlier, I believe both sides have much to offer and we're all stronger when each gender complements the other. And until we reach that nirvana of total understanding between the sexes, we all have to deal with these male and female "culture conflicts" in the workplace.

Perhaps no one personifies the struggle with this conflict better than Marlene, an independent television producer. On the one hand, when she's managing a project, Marlene says she has to spend a great deal of her time getting female subordinates to understand the concept of "it's not personal," when male executives behave aggressively or play the "I win. You lose." game.

"I think women tend to take it all way too personally," she says. "I can't tell you how frustrating it is to me, as a boss, to deal with the women who report to me who are always taking things personally. I'll tell them, 'Look, he wasn't singling you out personally by being demanding. *He treats everyone that way!*'"

On the other hand, when a long-time male colleague, Ben, cut Marlene out of a project that she hoped to work on, she found she had a very different attitude. "I felt betrayed," Marlene says now. "For a long time I didn't take things personally, especially the countless little things that happen at work. But after several years of it all building up, it really got to me. So yes, I did take what Ben did personally—but to a certain degree I knew I was consciously *choosing* to take it that way."

Like Marlene, perhaps you too have had to sort out conflicting thoughts and feelings about male behavior in the workplace. Your intellect may be telling you, "It's just business," while at the same time, your emotions are screaming, "It's personal!"

To help you run the rapids between those two positions, I'd like to share some of the exercises I use in my seminars.

### Dealing with Teasers and "Toppers"

As discussed throughout this chapter (and as seen in the examples of one-upmanship in Chapter 3) men bond by challenging each other in mock battles that establish the hierarchy in their relationships. These challenges often take the form of teasing one another or coming out with a "topper"—some statement that "tops" what the other guy has said or done.

This aspect of male behavior is something I had to teach my daughters about when they were still very young. I especially remember when one of my daughters came home distraught over an incident with a boy that occurred on the playground at school. When I asked why she was so upset, she proceeded to tell me how mean the little boy was to her.

"What did he do that made you so upset?" I asked. My daughter replied: "I was playing nicely with my friends, and he came and said my hair looked funny!" She had just had a haircut and, obviously, this did not go over very well with her.

I explained to her that little boys tease each other when they like someone.
"That's stupid," she replied.
"Yes, perhaps it is" I said. "But to the little boy, he thought he was being friendly. That's the way he plays with his friends. He didn't mean to hurt your feelings."
"Oh" she answered, "but it's still stupid!"
"The next time he teases you, tease him back," I suggested.

A few days later, the same boy started teasing my daughter, and she returned the favor. The little boy laughed and they both had a great time bantering back and forth. She had found a new best friend and learned a valuable lesson: *It really wasn't personal.*

Years later, I saw this same kind of dynamic play out in a corporate sales seminar I was leading. A female executive was giving a presentation and one of the slides showed a misspelled word that conveyed a completely different and humorous take on the original meaning. She noticed the mistake, apologized for it, and made a joke about the mixed message. The group chuckled along with her. It so happened that during that time, she was also taking night classes for her MBA. During the laughter, one of the men in the group remarked: "A lot of good the MBA is doing!"

The remark was not nice per se, but it is my contention that it was not personal in the sense that it was directed at her because she was a woman. Most likely the guy said it because he wanted to increase his status by putting someone down. She just happened to be a female.

My other contention was that he wasn't even conscious of the putdown. I verified this later when I commented to him that the remark seemed a bit caustic. He was truly stunned. "Oh," he said, "I was just teasing her. I have great respect for her and her ambition. I think she's great!" He later apologized to the executive.

In many ways the remark was a compliment, for men don't tend to tease or interact with people they don't like or respect. This one-up/one-down treatment is the method men use to bond with people they consider part of the team: people they like, trust and respect. Some women, on the other hand, use teasing as an indirect way to communicate what they really think—because they do not want to say something openly and directly. For these women, teasing is a passive/aggressive tactic, so when they are on the receiving end of it, they may bristle and take things personally—especially if a male is delivering the teasing remarks.

### Reality: Subject to Interpretation
As the story of the man who teased the female executive illustrates, a comment that a male considers "teasing" could easily be interpreted by the woman as a personal insult.

I want you to pay close attention to that word "interpreted," because it is one of the main contact points where male and female business cultures collide. (Actually, misinterpretation of another person's actions and communications is the source of most inter-personal conflicts and even wars—but we're not going to try to achieve world peace in this book just yet.)

To dig into this issue of interpretations, I'd like to start with giving humanity the benefit of the doubt and assume that people are doing the best they can given their own fears, desires, hopes and dreams. Each one of us has our own perceptions and beliefs about the world, and we act as if other people see the world in the same way we do. Essentially, we all view life through our own belief filters, and on top of that, each gender adds its own layer of filters. Men see the world through their male glasses and think that's how it *is*; and women see it through their female lenses and think *their* perception is the correct one.

Conflicts arise when an event takes place and we perceive it as different from our beliefs. To our old primal brains, different equals danger. And we frantically attempt to reduce this danger by lashing out at another, ignoring them and so on. When you experience someone belittling or dismissing you, rest assured they are reacting to *their* internal beliefs, and not to *you*! You are merely a spectator. In other words: It's not personal. Or as Hamlet says to Rosencrantz: *"...there is nothing either good or bad, but thinking makes it so."*

Bringing some of these lofty ideas down into our everyday work lives, let's look at how our interpretations of reality play out.

Suppose you greet your boss in the morning with a smile and a friendly "Hello!" He, in turn, responds with a Scrooge-like grunt, or worse, he looks right through you as though you aren't there, before going into his office and closing the door behind him.

Now most people would feel justified in interpreting the actions of the boss as being rude. But was he? Really?

If you look at the *action*, all that happened was that the boss failed to respond to a greeting—or at least he did not respond in the manner you expected him to.

But you could add any number of meanings to that event in giving it your own interpretation. You could think:

- "Boy, he's grumpy today. I'm going to stay out of sight."
- "What a jerk! How dare he treat me like that! I'll show him. I'll pretend I don't hear him the next time he starts talking to me."
- "Oh no! What have I done wrong? I am so stupid. I should have known better than to say anything to him first thing in the morning. He's ready to fire me, I know it!"

With this simple example, you can see how we might get carried away and let our interpretations take us down a path that has nothing to do with the reality of the situation.

Let's look at another example to see how our perceptions and expectations reflect our interpretation of reality.

Suppose you hear the words, "You're pregnant!" How do you interpret that news? If you're happily married and have wanted a child for a long time, you'll react with joy. But suppose you're an unwed teen who's just broken up with her boyfriend? How do you hear those words then? Or, what if you already have three children and you're in danger of losing your job? The words "You're pregnant!" are the same, but do you see how they can be interpreted in several different ways?

Remember—people's words and actions are not personal. They are responding to you based on what it means to *them*. It's never about you, it's always about them. Something in your words or actions triggered something within themselves that they are reacting to. Conversely, you are reacting to what another's communication means to you and not to the communication itself.

Here are a couple of exercises to help you apply these ideas in your work life:

## EXERCISE: Reinterpreting Reality

In this exercise, you will be imagining several different interpretations that you could give to a comment or action. Open up your mind to free associate and imagine a variety of possible responses you might have to a situation from work. Then write your answers in the "Your Turn" section.

## Example:
*This is what happened:*

My boss told me: "You could do better…"

(That's it! My boss uttered the phrase: "You could do better…" That is all that happened. Everything else is your story about what those words mean!)

*These are possible interpretations of what happened (your stories):*

- *Invalidation:* "He's saying I'm no good. I never can do things right! What's wrong with me?"

- *Anger:* "He thinks I could do better… Oh yeah! Look who's talking… He's such a loser!"

- *Curious\*:* "I wonder what he means? I'm going to ask him to see if there's something I can do to improve."

*\*Tip:* Adopting a curious interpretation puts you in a much stronger position than almost any other reaction, and curiosity is one of my favorite ways of being. When someone says or does something that could be interpreted as dismissive or rude, I become curious and say to myself: "Wow! That's different. I wonder what's going on with them to cause them to act that way. I think I'll ask (nicely) about what's going on." This approach gives me a different perspective and causes me to put my attention on the other person, not on me. There is an added benefit, too. The other person feels heard and acknowledged. (You can explore this idea further as you continue this exercise below.)

**Your Turn:**

Think of an incident at work that upset you. Now see if you can give it three or four different interpretations. Write your responses below:

*This is what happened:* _____

_____

_____

_____

_____

*These are my interpretations of what happened (or—This is what I say it means):* _____

_____

_____

_____

_____

When you have finished writing a few responses, go back and think about the incident again. Do you still feel upset about it? Do you feel a little less attached to your initial interpretation? If not, can you think of another way to look at what happened that might be less upsetting? Play with this exercise and use it whenever you need to get some perspective on events that you may be taking too personally.

You can also go one step further with this idea of "reinterpreting reality," and use this next exercise to become a more confident communicator.

**EXERCISE: Taking Control—The Power of Choose™**
In this exercise you will be giving a workout to your "choice muscle." It may feel awkward at first because you may have not used it in this way before. But as you go through the scenarios below, you'll begin to see that you have other choices besides simply reacting emotionally or taking things too personally at work.

**Example:**
*1. Think of something that upsets you and state how you feel about it.*
  "When he talks to me in that tone of voice, I feel hurt."

*2. Now add the word "choose" to the sentence.*
  "When he talks to me in that tone of voice I *choose* to feel hurt."

Notice how the word "choose" gives you back the power you have always had. It is your choice as to how you feel about anything that happens to you. (Would everyone feel hurt upon hearing those words? Obviously not. How you or anyone for that matter reacts to the words is a personal choice. Why not allow yourself other choices?)

*3. Substitute a new way of feeling that differs from the one you have already expressed, for example: I feel excited, curious, silly, or whatever other positive feeling you could have. Then restate the sentence using your new choice.*

- "When he talks to me in that tone of voice, I *choose to feel curious* and will ask him to clarify his statement so that I can better understand what he means."

**Your Turn:**

In the spaces below, complete the sentence using examples from your life and learn to take back what you have always had: control of your thoughts and feelings!

*1. Think of something that upsets you and state how you feel about it.*

When he/she (says, does, acts, etc.) _____

_____, I feel _____

_____.

*2. Now add the word "choose" to the sentence.*

When he/she (says, does, acts, etc.) _____

_____,

I *choose* to feel _____

_____.

*3. Substitute a new way of feeling that differs from the one you have already expressed, for example: I feel excited, curious, silly, or whatever other positive feeling you could have. Then, restate the sentence using your new choice.*

When he/she (says, does, acts, etc.) _____

_____,

I *choose to feel* (insert new feeling)_____

_____.

The more you make these conscious choices, the more opportunity you will have to feel the power returning to its rightful owner: YOU!

**Tip:** You can also apply this exercise to any negative feelings you have, as in this example:
1. "When I think about asking for a raise, I feel nervous."
2. "When I think about asking for a raise, I *choose* to feel nervous."
3. "Now when I think about asking for a raise, I *choose to feel confident* because I am well prepared, I do a good job, and I deserve that raise!"

Remember, you can always continue to choose to feel the old negative way anytime you want. In fact, decide from time to time to feel that way just for old time's sake. You will find that it doesn't have the same appeal it once had!

Marlene, the TV producer, shared her insights with me on how she applies some of these types of exercises in her own career. "One of the biggest things I interact with in the workplace is when people add their interpretations to something that happened," she said. "It's the meaning you add on to what happened that causes you to take something personally. But if you can step back from the event (or use some of the exercises) to help you see that it's just your interpretation of it—then it's a lot easier to not take things personally."

### *Just Because You Don't Take It Personally Doesn't Mean You Have to Take It*

Having raised your awareness about your personal perceptions of reality and perhaps, having gotten you to the point of acknowledging that everything that happens at work is not personal, I'm going to give you one caveat: If someone is abusive, don't accept it.

You don't always have to turn the other cheek. There are times when you *do* need to call the other person on their behavior. When someone says or does something that is out of line, stand your ground and assertively deal with it right away.

Here's a story that Deborah, a retired vice president, related to me showing how she dealt with a male in her office whose personal behavior crossed the line into abusive territory:

"There was one senior manager in a company I worked for who was known for being hot-tempered and yelling. People cowered when he behaved in this unacceptable way because of his position. There was one conversation I had with him in his office where I was not agreeing with him. He got red-faced. His voice got louder and he started getting huffy and puffy. I sat up in my chair and raised myself up a bit to increase my height. I leaned forward on the desk, and in as calm and hypnotic a voice as I could muster, I said: 'I know that you are very upset that we don't see things the same way; however, you may not speak to me in that tone of voice or use that kind of language.' Silently, I sat down, waiting until he got normal again—which he did. The lesson from that incident is that quiet strength can be a very powerful tool, even more powerful than loud arguments."

Virginia, a CEO who has done business with some of the most exclusive corporate boards in the country, offered this advice:

"Take note of how the particular man interacts with his wife/girlfriend. This woman has significant power in the man's life (if it is a normal/good relationship.) He has given her 'partnership' status. Watch how she communicates with him and incorporate that style into your approach to talking with him about important issues. (For example, some wives are formal, serious, and businesslike; some are smiling and soft spoken; some are opinionated and challenging.) This technique of mimicking the style a man is used to heeding from a woman has been very useful to me. But—and this is important—if you observe that the man is abusive, dismissive, and inconsiderate to his wife, then your chances of being treated with respect and fairness in your business relationship with him are fairly slim. If anything, do NOT mimic her behavior, as it will encourage similarly bad behavior on his part."

**Author's Comments:** Just because he treats his wife or girlfriend badly does not mean that he will necessarily treat you the same way. More than likely he treats his partner that way because she lets him for whatever unconscious reason.

There is a truism that says: "People treat you the way you teach them to treat you." In many cases the partner has allowed this behavior. You don't have to!

In the section on assertive communication you will learn how to teach the person how to treat you. If the person refuses, you have three choices:

1. Leave,
2. Put up with it (not an option in my opinion) or
3. Issue an ultimatum; "If this happens again, this is the consequence (legal action, HR, etc.)!" Then make sure you follow through!

### *The Choice Is Yours*

In explaining the win-lose credo of male business culture, it is not my intent for you to passively accept its rules. Rather, my aim throughout this discussion is to give you a chance to step back and take an objective view of some of the emotionally charged situations you encounter in the business world. Ultimately, by using some of the exercises and advice in this chapter, you will be able to make the best choices in your career or business.

Glenda, who worked in a high-tech company where screaming matches were the norm, found that she wasn't fazed by them and earned promotion after promotion. "When tempers flare," she observed, "the men just seem able to work through it, and the women who make it to upper management can endure it. But if you've never been exposed to that behavior, it's easy to take it personally—when it's not meant that way. You just have to decide if you can deal in a culture like that.

If you can, great. But if you can't, then it's probably not the place for you. You need to make the choice."

Susan, however, reached a point where she decided, "enough is enough." She left a lucrative position behind. "I finally said, 'OK. So it's not personal. He does that to everybody.' But—that doesn't mean I want to put up with it. When you get to the point where you can see that it's not personal to you, then it allows you to make decisions from a more powerful place—because you're not just reacting. You can say, 'That's just how he is, and he's not the kind of person I want to work with.' "

Just as Glenda and Susan demonstrate, not everyone will make the same choices. Ideally, we'd all like to work in companies where we acknowledge the strengths of both genders and minimize the weaknesses; businesses where women take things less personally while men develop more empathy for the female position and stop expecting them to "just get over it." Maybe then, we can move beyond the workplace struggles that keep us from enjoying the next game!

***When Men— or Women—Don't Move on to the Next Game.***
The general rule or credo in male business culture is "I win. You lose. Next game!™" But that doesn't mean that every man adheres to that motto. Some men *do* take things personally, and they don't let go after a fight—usually because they've not only lost the battle but because they've also lost face. They may complain constantly about their jobs or create an angry, caustic atmosphere at work. It is a safe bet that men, who hold grudges, complain all the time, get and stay angry have another issue going on; poor self esteem. A normal well-adjusted male will shake off a setback and get back in the game.

In extreme cases, these disgruntled men act out nightmare scenarios where they arm themselves with guns and shoot up their workplaces. Women, in general, tend to turn their frustrations and anger inward. They may take too many sick days or not enough; drive themselves into ulcers or breakdowns. If you are a co-worker to people who can't seem to let go when they "lose" (or if you are managing this type of employee), you will have to carefully assess the situation to decide on the best course of action. In some cases, you might be able to share some of the exercises in this book that are designed to give you some distance and perspective on events at work. Or you may want to share the idea that "it's not personal," and talk about how you relate to that concept. In any situation where you are seriously concerned about your safety, or that of other employees, you should, of course, discuss the matter with an appropriate manager or someone in the Human Resources department. For the most part, however, you will not be faced with such a dramatic challenge. More likely, you will have to deal with the "garden variety" frustration that arises among men when they are in the one-down position. As I've pointed out, most men know that they will have a chance to move up when it's time for the "next game." And for those who forget that they will have these opportunities, you can take steps to make sure they don't "lose face" publicly. Remember, for men, a loss of status is akin to an "emotional death."

## BRAIN (See Appendix)
### Hippocampus

Located in the medial temporal lobe, the hippocampus is part of the body's limbic system, and its job is to regulate emotion and memory. In her book, *The Female Brain*, Dr. Louann Brizendine calls the hippocampus "The elephant that never forgets a fight, a romantic encounter, or a tender moment." It is larger and more active in women—which may be one reason it is harder for females to move on to the "next game," as do men, or to forget an angry confrontation in the workplace.

## Chapter 5: Take a Risk

Everyone at the meeting knew Jason wasn't up to the job. But that didn't stop the 25-year-old from stepping up and saying he would spearhead research for a new product launch.

Clarice had asked for a volunteer to take on the project, and she didn't want to dampen his enthusiasm; after all, Jason was a new member of her department and fresh out of college. Yet she had seen this act before. Inwardly, she shared the unspoken assessment of two senior members of the team who rolled their eyes when Jason volunteered, because they all knew the job wasn't a good fit for someone with his limited experience.

On top of that, it had taken Clarice several years to rise to her current position as Department Head, and in that time she had experienced any number of run-ins with male co-workers who promised more than they could deliver and "bit off more than they could chew." At the same time, Clarice admired the ability of the men in her company to take risks and go where angels feared to tread. Properly guided, this "go for it" mentality produced some great products and ideas. Unguided, it could lead to disaster—and other people in the company (often the women, it seemed to Clarice) would have to clean up after those disasters. How many late evenings had she worked when her old boss couldn't pull off some grand project that he'd taken on in his bid for a higher status job in the company? (See more on this issue in *"The risk takers clean-up crew" at the end of the chapter*)

Clarice had no intention of letting this project fall prey to the over-reaching of a young staffer, so she chose her words carefully in response: "I like your enthusiasm Jason," she said. "That 'can do' attitude is vital to our success and I certainly want you to be part of the team. And, as this is such a big undertaking, I'd like to have John, Kumar and Shelly join you…"

Heads nodded in agreement with Clarice's proposal and she moved on to the next items on her agenda, feeling satisfied that she'd rewarded Jason for his risk-taking while at the same time ensuring that the project would stay on track.

### Acting "As If"

You might attribute Jason's over-eagerness to his youth. But I contend that it has much more to do with his gender. How many times have you been in a business meeting—or perhaps a social setting—when someone asks if anyone knows how to do something, like fix a Power Point projector or re-light a barbeque? Out of the blue, one man says he can handle the job: "Give it to me... I can do it... no problem at all." The only thing is, you *know* this man, and you also know *he does not have a clue about how to do it!*

Why in the world would he say such a thing, let alone volunteer for the task? Why would a man—whether he's a contractor or a consultant—claim a competency he *doesn't* have, while a woman will often downplay the very real abilities she *does* have?

The answer is because the men are practicing the art of "acting as if" they know how to do something.

From a young age, boys realize that the way to get noticed and selected for a sports team or a fun adventure is to make themselves known. In the competitive male world of "I win, you lose," men know they have to step forward and take risks if they are going to earn any rewards. So even if they are not exactly sure how to do something, or they've never done it before, men will "act as if" they can meet a challenge, because it provides them an opportunity to "win" and to gain status among the other males.

Plus—and this is important for women to understand— they will be respected by the other men *just for trying*. For instance, the scrawny kid who says he'll take on blocking Bruno—the 6' 6" halfback on an opposing football team—

earns admiration and respect from his team members. While they know the kid will probably get plowed under; he scores big points for taking the risk. And his status in the group goes up. The more a man "goes for it," the higher he can rise in the male hierarchy. (Men, too, will eventually stop awarding points to someone who repeatedly takes stupid chances. For the most part, males give more respect to a person who takes risks than they would to someone who does nothing at all.)

In this next section, we'll look more closely at how this approach to risk-taking became imbedded in the male psyche.

### A Good Hunter: Had to be Able to Take Risks

At this point, you may be able to recognize how the survival strategies of the *Homo sapiens* hunter still echo in the minds of modern men. In Chapter 2, we examined the need for those hunters to maintain a single focus in order to capture large prey—a trait reflected in the preference by today's males for targeted, bullet-point communication over long, detailed explanations. Chapter 3 showed how the hunters had to fight to be the best to earn the chance to reproduce, and how they fell in line behind the best hunter by establishing a one-up/one-down pecking order among the other males (Chapter 4) –dynamics that are also seen in corporate hierarchies and the win-lose approach to business competition.

Now, in trying to understand the male propensity for taking risks, it might seem obvious to point out that ancient hunters had to take huge chances when they attempted to kill large beasts that were much bigger and stronger than they were. If your choice is to throw a spear at a charging animal or be eaten by that animal, you are probably going to be inclined to try your luck with the spear. The *H. sapiens* males who took risks got fed, and those who didn't, starved. It could be argued that men are still taking risks to put food on the table. Look at those who sign up for physically dangerous jobs as police officers, fire fighters or oilrig roustabouts, as well as the men who go after financially risky challenges as entrepreneurs or hedge-fund managers.

It may seem logical, therefore, that some men are driven to take risks because they see direct rewards—mates, food and/or fortune—on the horizon. But I'd like to pull back the curtain on male behavior a little further to help you understand the route men take to get to those rewards. As much as we glorify the accomplishments of the lone individual in this society, the fact is that most grand accomplishments—whether building the pyramids or launching the moon shot—require teams of people working together. Men understand that the path to success lies in making the team. And a man also knows that the first step toward that goal is to be sure he stands out as an individual with unique skills and talents. He not only wants to get *on* the team, he also needs to *make himself indispensable* to that team.

In ancient times, males distinguished themselves primarily because their survival depended on it. Suppose four guys in your *H. sapiens* clan were pretty good at hefting a rock toward a wooly mammoth. If two of them got trampled underfoot in the hunt, that still left two rock throwers. Sad, but not such a big deal in terms of survival. Let's further suppose, however, that you developed an extraordinary sense of tracking and you could point the other hunters to the best spot for finding prey. If the clan lost you under the mammoth's hoofs, then your crucial skills as a tracker would be lost too. You and your special skill, therefore, became much more valuable to the group, and you certainly improved your status among the males. (See the section on *"Rudolph the Red-Nosed Risk Taker"* at the end of the chapter)

The bottom line is that no *H. sapiens* males wanted to be perceived as "disposable." As mentioned in the Introduction, the death of a single woman in pre-historic society could have a major impact on the survival of the group. But men were slightly more expendable, because only a few males were actually needed to insure reproduction.

The need to be seen as vital to the group, rather than superfluous, is one of the driving forces behind male risk-taking, according to Dr. Roy Baumeister, a psychology professor at the University of Florida. In a 2007 address to the American Psychological Association entitled "Is There Anything Good About Men," Dr. Baumeister pointed out that "… being different is a vital strategy for belonging to a large group." He went on to say, "If you are the only group member who can kill an antelope or find water or talk to the gods or kick a field goal, the group can't afford to get rid of you."

In a nutshell, that's why males take risks and why young Jason raised his hand to volunteer for a job he wasn't remotely ready to handle: men don't want to be kicked off the team. They don't want the group to get rid of them. Along with the bragging and boasting men do about things they've already accomplished (see Chapter 3), they will also stretch out into the unknown to take risks and show the other guys what they might yet accomplish in the future. They are signaling that they can help the team win.

In my mind, it's crucial for women to understand how this works. Much of what happens in business revolves around men, impressing other men and it usually has nothing to do with the women in the office. As I've said before: it's not personal. If you're old enough to remember the Van Morrison song, "Wild Nights," you may recall a line in it that said, "… all the girls go by dressed up for each other." Just as the girls are seeking to impress the other girls in that song, so, too, do the "boys" seek approval from other males. If you switch the genders in that song, it might go like this: "… all the boys take risks just to show off for each other!"

So the men earn benefits from touting their special individual skills and standing out in the pack—all to avoid being kicked off the team and out into the cold. Again, quoting Dr. Baumeister's talk; "Men create the kind of social networks where individuals are replaceable and expendable. Women favor the kind of relationships in which each person is precious and cannot truly be replaced." And he also points out, "… Men think of themselves based on their unusual traits *that set them apart* from others, while women's self-concepts feature things *that connect them* to others."

Because women tend to put more emphasis on connectedness and cooperation, they are less likely to follow the male model of rewarding those who try to stand out in the crowd. Let's not forget too, that while the *Homo sapiens* males gained status for taking chances, the primary responsibility for the females was to care for vulnerable young children, which made them more risk-averse. Female brains, too, are less geared toward impulsivity and risk-taking. (See the *"Brain Basics"* section at the end of the chapter)

Yet women, like men, are not slaves to their ancestral heritage and brain chemistry. They can overcome any personal aversion to risk-taking, as many trail-blazing women have proven—especially in the last couple of decades as women have established themselves in a variety of formerly male-dominated jobs, from becoming Congresswomen and CEOs to astronauts and television anchors.

Nevertheless, many of the women I meet in my seminars still have a difficult time when it comes to stretching beyond their comfort zones and taking on challenges in their workplaces and businesses. To give you new tools for strengthening your risk-taking abilities, in the next sections, I will share examples and exercises that have helped women, independent of the phase of her career.

## You Are Truly Exceptional!

In terms of risk-taking, we've seen how men "act as if" they can do something—whether they can or not—because it helps them increase their status and stand out from the rest of the pack. I wouldn't suggest you try that strategy because it's not likely to be authentic for you.

I will encourage you, however, to start giving yourself more credit for the things you *are* capable of, and what you have *already* achieved. Remember, men are ready to present (OK ... to boast) about their accomplishments at any time in order to win the one-up/one-down contest inherent in many male interactions. Women, on the other hand, do not usually keep a laundry list of their achievements in the back of their minds to call up on a moment's notice. Additionally, women tend not to appreciate how an achievement in one arena can be transferred to another.

When I worked with Lorena, for instance, and we did the "Exceptional You!" exercise (which follows later in this section), she told me, initially, that she had not really done anything out of the ordinary in her life. She said she was "…just an IT consultant." As we talked further, she revealed that she was caring for her aged mother in addition to raising her own family. I found that extraordinary! As we probed further into what she actually did every day, we came up with a long list of accomplishments and capabilities. Think of the attention to detail and patience needed to care for her mother. Think of the incredible management skills she developed and used to make sure everyone in her family was taken care of. She also had an amazing ability to remain calm in the face of all of it.

After thinking about her daily life, Lorena began to realize that the demands of her work world—upset people, tight deadlines and unreasonable demands—were really no different than the kinds of challenges she was taking in stride in her personal life. Viewed from that angle—and acknowledging her "transferable achievements"—she realized that anything that happened at work was a "piece of cake." As she began to acknowledge how capable she really was, Lorena's confidence grew to the point where she doubled her fees and expanded her business, simply because she stopped and recognized the strengths she already possessed.

In my own life, I went through a process similar to Lorena's, when I discovered that I had capabilities beyond those I thought I had. It started when I quit smoking. I began smoking when I was in my early teens, having an occasional cigarette with my fellow classmates. A year or two later, however, I found myself smoking almost four packs a day! These weren't light, filtered cigarettes, but Camel cigarettes—unfiltered. One day, I finally had enough. Cigarettes were getting expensive, my clothes reeked of smoke, my fingers were stained, and I was beginning to get a cough. I decided to quit, cold turkey. I have to admit that it was one of the hardest things I have ever had to do. Now, more than 25 years later, I still think about lighting up! That's how addicted I was to tobacco.

Several years after I quit and I was raising my two young daughters, I remember dropping one of my girls off at daycare. At the time, I was still feeling devastated about the divorce, worried over a job that was slowly phasing out, and overwhelmed with feelings of inadequacy about bringing up my daughters alone. As I was leaving the daycare center, I noticed a woman anxiously lighting a cigarette. Suddenly, I was reminded of my own days of smoking and the hell I had experienced quitting. I remember feeling sorry for the woman. But I simultaneously felt a sense of pride in my strength in quitting. The more I thought about it, the better I began to feel—not because she was still smoking and I wasn't—but because I took action and quit.

I realized that if I was able to stop smoking, I could do anything I put my mind to! From that moment on, I knew I could handle whatever came my way. If I had the power to stop smoking, I had the power to raise my daughters. I could handle work, regardless of what happened. I must be incredible! Now, I'm not saying this in the spirit of male boasting but to share with you the genuine realization that was a turning point in my life—a point when I realized that I actually had far more strength than I ever knew I had.

I began to apply the lessons I had learned from quitting cigarettes to the challenges of parenthood. First of all, no matter how stressful things got (and they did, especially in the teenage years!), I knew that life would get better if I continued to tap into the inner resolve that enabled me to kick tobacco. I began stretching out of my comfort zone and taking more risks. I started using meditation again to relax and taught my girls that practice, as well. To get my mind off cigarettes, I took up gourmet cooking. I shared this knowledge with my daughters as a way for us to spend time together.

I was beginning to understand the idea that I not only had transferable skills, but also to give myself credit for having "transferable achievements." I remember one time when I was in the store with one of my girls and she wanted a special doll. I told her that perhaps Santa would bring it to her for Christmas. Well, that was not acceptable to her! She wanted it there and then and proceeded to have a meltdown in the middle of the store. My first reaction was to get into a big confrontation with her and let her know who was boss. But sanity prevailed, and I decided on a different tact. I let her express her disappointment (actually her rage) while gently telling her that I understood how upset she was. I told her that as a little boy, I too, was angry when I couldn't get a toy truck that I wanted so badly. After a few minutes, her anger subsided and she became her normal cheerful self. Because I validated her feelings (they were *her* feelings, after all), she felt heard and understood. We became a little closer as a result. I cannot imagine that I would have handled the situation in that way if it had happened right after the divorce when I was scared and anxious about being a single parent. But once I had built my confidence as a parent by piggybacking on my experience as someone who had quit smoking, I was able to remain calm with my daughter when she was screaming her head off.

Now I ask you, how is dealing with an upset kid in a toy store any different from dealing with an angry coworker? If I could placate a screeching child, surely I could do the same with an irate boss. When I faced difficult people or work situations, I'd tell myself "You've handled it before, you can handle it now!"

I could go on about how my experience in quitting smoking gave me incredible resources to use in other areas of my life.

But I trust you're getting the idea. And just as I found out, you, too, have knowledge and capabilities that you don't realize you possess. What happens to us, however, is that when we face situations that are unfamiliar or stressful, we tend to forget the many ways we have already been successful in handling similar situations in the past. We shrink from risk and say we're afraid to take a chance on something new. Our minds fool us by telling us that since the context or circumstances are different in this new situation, and then our past experience doesn't matter. Nothing could be further from the truth. You *are* capable. You *are* exceptional. And you don't have to be afraid of taking a risk. I invite you to do this next exercise to see for yourself that what I'm saying is true.

## EXERCISE: Exceptional You!

This exercise is designed to counteract the tendency of many women to forget or discount their numerous accomplishments. This tendency can hold you back and make you less likely to take risks that could advance your career or expand your business. Because you are pushing against ingrained thought patterns in your mind, it is important to do this exercise when you have 30 uninterrupted minutes to devote to it. It will change your life!

### *Exceptional You! Part 1:*

In the space below or in a separate notebook, start writing every personal accomplishment you can think of: speaking in front of a group, graduating from school, raising children, earning a promotion, starting a business, learning a new skill, quitting smoking…anything. Also, be sure to write down everything and anything you do in life, from getting out of bed in the morning and brushing your teeth, to navigating the freeway and coping with office mates. As you write, just let it flow. Don't worry about spelling, grammar or punctuation. Don't second guess yourself or comment on the significance of some achievement. Just write. *And keep writing continuously for at least 10 minutes without stopping.* Don't pick your pen up from the paper throughout those 10 minutes. If nothing comes to mind, just doodle or write anything you can think of until another accomplishment pops into your consciousness. Now go!

_____

_____

_____

_____

_____

_____

_____

_____

_____

_____

_____

_____

_____

_____

_____

_____

_____

Read over what you have written. Give yourself permission to really see all the incredible things you have accomplished. Resist the temptation to downplay them. Even getting up and going to work is a big deal, for there are plenty of people who don't.

### *Exceptional You! Part 2:*

Next, write down one accomplishment from Part 1 of this exercise in the space below. After that, list the strengths and abilities you demonstrated in this achievement. Finally, list areas where you can use this strength or ability. Then list additional accomplishments from Part 1 and repeat this process for each one.

**Accomplishment** (from Part 1):

**Example:** *Quit smoking.*

**Your Turn:** _____

_____

_____

_____

_____

_____

_____

## What strengths and/or abilities did you demonstrate by this accomplishment?

**Example:** *Ability— to handle an extremely difficult personal challenge; Ability— to commit to my well-being; Strength— resisting a habitual behavior in favor of more productive choices.*

**Your Turn:** _____

_____

_____

_____

_____

## Where can I use this strength and/or ability in other areas of my life?

**Example:** *I can use these strengths and abilities when I deal with difficult people at work, and I can be more productive because I know how to make the best choices for myself.*

**Your Turn:** _____

_____

_____

_____

_____

Now choose another accomplishment from your list and repeat the process.

**Accomplishment** (from Part 1):
**Your Turn:** _____

_____

_____

_____

_____

_____

_____

**What strengths and/or abilities were demonstrated by this accomplishment?**

**Your Turn:** _____

_____

_____

_____

_____

_____

_____

_____

# Where can I use this strength and/or ability in other areas of my life?

**Your Turn:** _____

_____

_____

_____

_____

_____

_____

This evaluation of your achievements should be an ongoing process. The more you use this exercise, the more you will realize how incredible and exceptional you really are—and the more willing you will be to take risks and stretch out of your comfort zone. I firmly believe that each of has all the resources we need within us, right now, to do whatever we want. We lack nothing. The knowledge you have within you right now is truly amazing. It is there waiting to be acknowledged and applied to the challenges you face every day.

## *But What if I Fail?*

Even though you've just inventoried your record of achievements and highlighted your strengths and abilities using the "Exceptional You!" exercise, you may still have a nagging little voice in the back of your head saying "But what if I fail?" I'm not going to pretend that you can get rid of that voice, because it comes with the package of being human.

I believe there is no such thing as "failure." If you look at the actual definition of the word, you will see that it means, "not achieving your desired end." In other words, the outcome that you *hoped for* or *wanted* didn't happen. That's all. Negative feelings and self-judgment are qualities we add to the meaning of the word "failure."

Instead of fearing "failure," why not view setbacks as opportunities to change what you're doing and try something different? What if you started to view a "failure" as a form of feedback that gives you information on how to get closer to your goal? When you take a risk, no one can guarantee the outcome. The good news, however, is that by taking action, you always receive information on how to accomplish your objectives. As long as you take action, you win. How cool is that?

Every time you take risks and take action, you grow stronger and more confident—regardless of whether you "fail" to get the desired outcome or not. Men tend to do this and it is one of the reasons they "act as if" they know how to do things. Men learn that by "acting as if," they gain confidence in their abilities. This leads them to attempt more and more feats of daring. Since they earn points and respect just for trying, there's no downside for them—and I contend there is no downside for you, as a woman, either. If your risk-taking moves turns out as you hoped, you win. And if your risk-taking doesn't go according to plan, you still win because you will have learned valuable lessons and can face the next challenge armed with that knowledge.

As the writer Rita Mae Brown says, "Good judgment comes from experience, and often experience comes from bad judgment." So go out and get some experience!

One other point about the differences in the way men and women approach risk is something you may have noticed already for yourself, and that is this: If a man takes a risk and comes up short, he often blames external forces—not himself! Of course not every male does this, but let me run a typical scenario by you to illustrate my point. Suppose a man gets lost while driving (Heaven forbid). Typically, he will start to blame things that are *outside his control* as the reason. Perhaps clouds prevented the GPS system from working properly, or new construction blocked the landmarks he was used to seeing, or the radio was too loud so he couldn't concentrate on where he was going, etc., etc. The reason men do this, you must remember, is that the need to maintain status is primal—which means that if something goes wrong it must be the fault of something or someone else. So, as I said before, there is little downside to risk-taking for men in most situations, because they can rise in status just for trying. If things don't work out, they can shift the blame elsewhere. I'm not suggesting or recommending that you follow this particular male behavior pattern. Just as men tend to blame external forces when their risk-taking does not pay off, women often turn the blame inward. They look for their internal faults and pronounce sentence on themselves for "failing"—whether they deserve that verdict or not! Not all women respond in this way, of course, but if you are one who does, I invite you to examine that behavior more closely, because it is not very productive.

Keep in mind, too, that men's brains provide an environment for compartmentalizing issues. If they take a risk that does not succeed, they can put it away in one box and separate it from the other boxes where they keep their self-esteem and confidence. Women, endowed with a larger hippocampus, have a harder time forgetting "failures." You will have to be alert to that tendency to hold on to mistakes, and practice letting them go, as most men are able to do. Other tactics that you can use from the male playbook can be found in the section on *"Mistakes and Missed Takes"at the end of the chapter.* You can further expand your ability to take risks by completing the following exercise.

## EXERCISE: Reevaluating Risks

In this simple exercise, you will take a look at some of your past experiences in risk-taking and give yourself credit for the times you were successful. If you judged yourself to be not successful after taking a risk; that is, if you considered yourself a "failure," then I want you to reevaluate what happened to see what you learned from the experience and how it might be useful to you going forward.

**Write a brief description of an event or experience of taking a risk in your career or business:**

**Example:** *In my company, when an opportunity appeared to manage a temporary administrative staffer, I volunteered to do it.*

**Your Turn:** _____

_____

_____

_____

_____

_____

_____

_____

_____

**What happened as a result of taking this risk?**

**Example:** *The temp worker was not qualified for the tasks and I ended up having to do the work that had been assigned to him.*

**Your Turn:** _____

_____

_____

_____

_____

_____

_____

_____

**How did you evaluate that result? Was it successful or not successful?**

**Example:** *I considered it to be unsuccessful, and I promised myself I'd never do that again. Let someone else have that headache.*

**Your Turn:** _____

_____

_____

_____

_____

_____

## Can you re-evaluate that risk now? What lessons did you learn? What did you learn from that experience?

**Example:** *I did learn that I do need to do a little more homework before I volunteer for a task. If I had asked a few more questions, I could have learned what was expected of both the temp and me. I could have managed him appropriately. I also saw that a co-worker who was successful in working with the temps was given more responsibilities and moved into management herself.*

**Your Turn:** _____

_____

_____

_____

_____

_____

_____

_____

_____

I purposefully provided you with a very simple example of a risk in this exercise, because I want you to apply it to the types of situations you actually face in your own workplace. Too many times, we talk about risk-taking in terms of scaling Mt. Everest or exploring the Amazon. In fact, very few of us actually need—or want—to take those "glamorous" risks. Instead, we may only need to stretch out far enough to be chosen as one of the team members on a new project or to earn a pay raise. It really doesn't matter whether the risks you need to take are large or small. The important thing is that you recognize what you need to do—and do it!

Beatrice, for instance, decided she would stop hanging back when her co-workers took part in a team-building exercise. As an executive assistant in her department, she usually stayed within her self-imposed role as the "photographer" of events, instead of being a participant. After one of my seminars, she decided that she would take a risk and step out of that role. "It was just a cooking class," Beatrice told me. "I decided that I would not just sit on the sidelines. Before, I would have held myself back and only taken pictures. I decided instead to jump in and be a part of the action. Since I cooked with everyone, suddenly I was on the team and that one class has made a huge difference in how I'm perceived and treated. It was worth the risk."

For Sarah, risking meant speaking up instead of retreating when presented with a chance to grow at work. An accomplished IT professional, with more than seven years of experience, Sarah had worked on a wide variety of projects, but she had never managed one. After doing the "Exceptional You!" exercise, and also looking at the lessons she learned from both successful and unsuccessful risk-taking, she decided it was time to spread her wings a bit. Several months after joining a new company, an opportunity arose where Sarah could take the lead and manage an entire project. At a staff meeting, Sean, the IT Director opened the floor for comments and suggestions about implementing a new program for the company that would have to be executed flawlessly.

"The silence was deafening," Sarah recalled, "but in that moment, I decided it was 'now or never.' I spoke up. I didn't just say I'd volunteer to lead the project, I also told them about how I had worked on a similar program at my previous company—and that I really knew what *not* to do. I didn't brag, but I did send the message that I had some achievements under my belt, and that I was willing to guide the team through this uncharted territory."

Impressed with the way she handled herself, and her willingness to take a risk, Sean named Sarah the team leader. Under Sarah's leadership' the project was completed without any major glitches and was deemed a resounding success by all. A year later, Sarah took over Sean's position as IT Director when he became a Vice President.

Perhaps you're in a position like Beatrice, where you need to take a small step into a new area. Or you could be like Sarah, and it's time for you to step up to the plate in a major way on a large challenge. Only you can define what level of risk you need in order to move forward. Or up, up, up…

You've learned, found and possibly experienced some new tools in this chapter that can help you go beyond any limitations you've set on yourself. And you also have something else that you've always possessed inner strength and knowledge waiting to be tapped. So take a risk. There's no time like now!

## The Risk-takers Cleanup Crew

When men take risks, they can earn a high status position among other males and they also get respect "just for trying." Even if they fail, the risk may still pay off. But men sometimes have another cushion that protects them from the downside of taking risks: women. The women in a company may end up being those who have to "clean up" after a man who makes a bold move. Joan was one of those women who had to be the backstop for risk-taking males in several entrepreneurial companies. "I've just had a few too many experiences of guys being "cowboys," she told me. "These guys think of themselves as risk-takers who shoot from the hip—but really, they just go off and do things the way they want to do them and ignore the negative consequences. They don't think things through, and then I've had to come in and clean up after them and make the project work anyway. They don't recognize and appreciate what I'm doing. They think they're successful doing things as they've always done them. But the only reason they've been successful is because they've had all these women underneath them cleaning things up behind them. I figured out that if I was going to have to do all that work anyway, I'd just as soon take my own risks. So I quit my job and started my own company!"

## Rudolph the Red-Nosed Risk Taker

Even though it's a silly, sentimental Christmas song, "Rudolph the Red-Nosed Reindeer" tells a great story about male business culture. (Assuming, of course, that Rudolph and the other reindeer in Santa's stable are male.) In the story of Rudolph, we see how much value is placed on each man's ability to demonstrate his unique, individual talents for helping the team win—and how men earn rewards and increase their status in the hierarchy by taking risks. If you recall, Rudolph's shiny red nose made him an object of scorn to the other reindeer that used to "laugh and call him names." That's how men treat other low-status males who have done nothing to prove themselves and establish their place in the pack. But then came that fateful "foggy Christmas Eve," when "Santa came to say: Rudolph with your nose so bright, won't you guide my sleigh tonight?" At last, Rudolph has a chance to stand out from the crowd and show how he, and he alone, could fulfill this important mission. His value to the group soars. Little Rudolph has presumably never been in a leadership role, but he takes the risk and leads the reindeer "team" to victory—while also putting smiles on the faces of children around the world. His reward: acceptance by the others ("...then how the reindeer loved him!") and high status in the pecking order. Plus his risk-taking earned him immortality—because as we all know Rudolph the Red-Nosed Reindeer went "down in his-to-ry!

## Mistakes and "Missed Takes"

While women can let their fear of making mistakes stop them from taking risks, men know that risks are just a part of life. Growing up, if males want to be picked for a sports team and excel on that team, they had to risk dropping the ball, getting knocked down and even ridiculed from time to time. They learned to accept disappointments as part of the game. So a mistake, from the male point of view, can be seen as a "missed take," a minor bump in the road, instead of a roadblock. Because of their brain structure, men can also let go of things more easily than women. So if a risk goes wrong, the men may simply say "FIDO"—which means "Forget It, Drive On."

## BRAIN (Appendix)

### Anterior Cingulate Cortex (ACC)

The Anterior Cingulate Cortex (ACC) of our brain is involved in weighing options and making decisions. It also detects errors and processes conflicts. Dr. Louann Brizendine calls it the "worry-wart" center in her book, *The Female Brain*. She also points out that the ACC is larger and more active in women than men. Small wonder, then, that women tend to be more risk-averse than men.

## Chapter 6: First THIINGS First!

When she was a teen coming of age as a feminist in the 1970s, Marian could never figure out why advertisers would pose a beautiful woman in an elaborate evening gown next to an ordinary car in a dealer's showroom.

"I just thought it was ridiculous," she recalls. "I mean, what woman in an evening dress would stand around next to a car in the middle of the day? It made no sense to me whatsoever. So I wrote it off as just one more example of sexist exploitation of women's bodies that you could always find in *Ms.* magazine back then."

Years later, while working as a copywriter at an advertising agency, a male friend explained the appeal of those car ads to Marian. "He told me something that's stuck with me," Marian says, "When men see those pictures, they think: 'If I buy this car, then I'll get that woman.' That was the message."

"I still think it's ridiculous," Marian adds, "because what are the chances that some schlubby guy will actually have a relationship with one of those supermodels? But at least now I understand the male thought process a little better. And I can see how it makes sense to the men on some level—even if *I* think it's stupid."

Marian's comments reminded me very much of the conversation I had with one of my daughters when I explained that the little boy on the playground wasn't really trying to be mean when he teased her about her new haircut. He was just one-upping her because that's the way he treated other boys, and he assumed that she'd like that treatment as well. After my explanation, my daughter also said, "That's stupid." But she accepted the fact that boys thought differently than she did and eventually made friends with the kid who teased her.

In Marian's story, we see not only the great gulf that exists between male and female perceptions, but we also get a glimpse into what's important to men. *Things*—not relationships—are the first priority for most males. If I get that car, *then* I get the woman. If I buy this expensive watch and show how successful I am, *then* I'll get a date. If I earn that raise, *then* my family will love me.

Just as men live by the motto, "I Win, You Lose, Next Game!™" so, too, do they adhere to the unconscious rule that states: "Things first, then people."

It's not that men are necessarily shallow and materialistic (well… maybe a little), rather, they are hard-wired to know they must first achieve before they can receive. Like high school students who understand they have to do their homework first before they get to go to the movies, males know they have to venture forth and slay the dragon before they get to kiss the princess.

Naturally, men tend to put things before people. And they learned to do that from their caveman ancestors.

### A Good Hunter: Must be Able to Manipulate Things

While the caveman's woman might keep him warm at night, having a sharper spear could be the thing to keep him from being killed by a wild animal. The *Homo sapiens* hunter, therefore, focused much of his attention on designing and developing better tools for the hunt. Out of necessity, he studied his environment and the movement of animals. Perhaps lengthening a spear shaft would result in a quicker kill, or tying tree limbs together might make a better trap. Early hunters recognized that the more they could understand about how things worked—and manipulate them in their favor—the better their chances for winning.

While the male hunters relied on each other, they mainly put their attention on tracking, stalking and killing the prey. Undoubtedly, the men formed rudimentary bonds with each other, but they were not like the relationships the women created. It was not important whether a member of the hunting party "liked" you or not, but whether he could be counted on to "watch your back" and contribute to the success of the hunt. In other words, was the person useful to the group?

The main work of the *H. sapiens* women, by contrast, was to insure the survival of their offspring. They had to focus on the human beings under their watch and foster connections with the other women who might also care for their babies and children. Relationships, then, took top billing among the females.

Apparently, this pattern from our earliest history is imprinted on females at their earliest stages of life. Researchers tell us that female infants instinctively focus on people, looking at their faces and listening to voice tones as a means to connect. During the first three months of life, a baby girl's ability to make eye contact and gaze at faces increases several fold, while that of infant boys does not increase at all. Guess what baby boys turn their most intense gazes upon? Objects. They're fascinated by bright balloons and flashing lights—*things*, not people.

For more details on this research, see the study by Rebecca Leeb and F. Gillian Rejsking, titled *"Here's looking at you, kid!"* published in the journal, *Sex Roles* (Volume 50, Nos. 1-2.)

Remember too, the female brain is wired for connectivity. Besides all of the links between the left and right hemispheres, the insula, the home of "social emotions" in the brain, is larger and more active in women than in men (see *"Brain Basics"* section at the end of the chapter for more details.) And this area of the brain gives rise to empathy, which may be one more reason females place a greater emphasis on relationships.

To most women, therefore, one of the catch phrases of best-selling author and financial guru, Suze Orman, makes sense. In stating her priorities, Orman says: "People first, then money, then things."

Men, too, want connections with others, financial success, and material possessions—they just pursue them in a different order than do women.

So while both genders want the same outcomes, the routes they take to those goals could not be more different—nor more fraught with potential conflict between the genders.

### Results not relationships...
One area of conflict that arises from the way males set priorities is that men often focus on "getting the job done" while sometimes running over the people doing the job.

Up to this point, I've given you the equation for male priorities as *"things* first, then people"—a truism that obviously applies to the many men who are gadget freaks and those who act like "boys with their toys" when they show off their latest cell phone or hot new golf putter. And today's technology certainly gives men lots of "things" to focus on instead of human beings.

But if we substitute the word "results" for the word "things" in our equation, you may get a better picture of what's going on with the men in your workplace or business: *results* first, then people. For starters, I don't think I'd get much argument with my contention that men in business tend to focus more on results than relationships. We spend more time talking about the "bottom line" and quarterly earnings than we do discussing the well-being of staff members. Of course the enlightened view today is that "people matter" and "we care" about employees and customers. Underneath all of that, however, echoes the voice of our ancestral grandfathers who remind us that our survival depends on our things, our tools, our results, and not so much on the people around us.

Imagine then, what happens when a results-oriented male manager (who puts "things" first and people second) tries to direct the work of a relationship-oriented female.

My friend, Gloria, experienced that conflict when she worked in a high-octane sales environment. "The only way I knew how to work was through relationships," Gloria recalls. "And through those relationships, I could ask people to do a lot of things."

"But most of the men managed off the numbers," she says. "They focused only on the target. When things got tight in the organization, my supervisor would come in and try to make me manage by hitting this number or that number. It never worked, and my results would go down."

"I couldn't just demand that people hit a target," Gloria adds. "That was never effective for me. I did it by encouraging people—empowering them and appreciating them. Then they were motivated to get the job done, and they wanted to produce the results for me." Even though Gloria's sales results were actually better when she did things her way, the company's managers insisted that she follow their protocols, so she finally left the job.

Unfortunately, women like Gloria are leaving the ranks of good companies every day because some men cannot quite grasp the value of this "female-oriented" approach to business. Sometimes this male blind spot can cause a company to lose more than a good employee. It can also mean the loss of huge sums of money.

This story, told by Patti, one of my seminar participants, is a prime example:

"Harry was this hard-charging vice president, and he went into negotiations with Donna, the CIO of a company that was dissatisfied with Harry's product. It turned out that the original sales person who set up the deal just glossed over some of the concerns of the people in Donna's company instead of addressing the problems early on. By the time Donna became involved, she was one unhappy customer. During the negotiations, Harry tried to throw money on the table to solve everything. He put all of his energy into creating a financial fix and offering a rebate instead of realizing that Donna's people were feeling hurt and distrustful. On top of that, Harry was being very aggressive and his attitude was 'Let's get this deal done… here are the terms, here's the money, just sign.' Meanwhile, Donna wanted more assurances and clarity about the contract. Her questions were 'How do I make sure my team gets what they need?' and, 'How do I make this a win-win?' Everything broke down because Harry was so focused on the result—closing the deal. He was tone deaf about the relationship issues and never addressed Donna's need to be sure her staff would be successful. That ended up costing Harry's company millions and millions of dollars in lost business."

### *Playing to Your Strengths*

As the stories from Gloria and Patti show, the traditional male focus on "results first" does not always produce the best outcome.

Women, however, can often provide an alternative to that traditional approach when they play to one of their strengths—and that is their ability to nurture relationships without sacrificing the bottom line. Rather than trying to replicate male management techniques, the successful women I know have all found their own unique ways of blending their relationship-building skills into their communication style at work.

Kelly, for instance, is a senior executive at a package delivery company, and she has to balance the need for her line managers to listen to employee problems while at the same time meeting hyper-fast deadlines.

"Sometimes," Kelly says, "a driver may be frustrated because his truck was not loaded exactly as it should have been and he just needs to vent. I work with our managers to train them to really listen to the drivers and let them blow off steam when necessary instead of saying 'Tough luck…go hit your route.' "

"There are other times," she adds, "when things are moving so fast that no one has time to listen. That's when I advise the managers to say they'll set up an appointment later to hear what the employee has to say. But when they do have those appointments, they have to genuinely listen. They can't just pay lip service to the idea of caring about the employee's point of view; they actually have to demonstrate that they hear it."

Gabriel, a participant in one of my seminars, does not have the same type of work challenges Kelly faces. Nevertheless, she too has used her sensitivity to relationship issues in productive ways.

She called one day to tell me about a situation with her boss, an executive, who was doing fairly well until being told that he was not communicating effectively with employees in the lower echelon of the company. "That's when I remembered what you said about men putting things (or results) first and people second," Gabriel told me. "I realized my boss was in the typical male mode of thinking 'Let's just get the job done,' and he wasn't paying attention to massaging the relationships."

"So," she said, "I came up with this idea… I started adding staff member's birthdays and their company anniversaries to his calendar. That way, he could send them a note to recognize the day."

"It turns out my boss is actually pretty sentimental," she added. "And when he sent out the emails or cards, it was a big hit with everyone on staff. People felt appreciated because he went out of his way and took the time to acknowledge them. I also made sure to put monthly and quarterly employee meetings on his calendar instead of waiting to have one annual meeting—that has made a big difference in our performance too."

"Your boss ought to give you a raise," I told Gabriel.

"He did!" she replied, laughing.

I'd be willing to bet that you, too, have applied your relationship-building abilities in positive ways in your workplace. You'll tap into those experiences in this next exercise.

## EXERCISE: Rewarding Relationships

Have you ever saved the day because you were sensitive to the personal issues of co-workers or employees? Has your capacity to connect to other people helped you in dealing with customers? Has it improved your company's bottom line?

Just as you listed your accomplishments in the "Exceptional You!" exercise in Chapter 4, you should acknowledge the times you've used your relationship-building skills at work. That way, you won't discount those experiences in the face of the results-driven in which culture we all work. By completing this exercise, you'll also have examples of these skills lined up in your mental portfolio, ready to call up when needed—for instance, if you have to defend your reasons for setting up a certain procedure or for taking the personal approach with a particular client.

*Instructions:* Think of a time when you put "people first and things second" that led to a rewarding experience at work. Describe what you did and how it turned out.

**Example:** *I knew that George could be resentful about my managing him because he's older and has been with the company much longer than I have. So I took him to lunch and asked his advice about the project we were working on. He felt appreciated and, even though we couldn't apply some of his ideas, he started participating more actively in our weekly meetings. I feel I created an ally out of someone who could have become an enemy.*

## Your Turn: _____

_____

_____

_____

_____

_____

_____

_____

_____

_____

_____

_____

_____

_____

_____

_____

_____

_____

_____

Use a separate piece of paper or a notebook to document repeats of this exercise and list several other examples of how you've created rewarding relationships at work. As with the "Exceptional You!" exercise, you can return to this list and expand it any time you wish.

Bethany, who works in the venture capital field, did this exercise at one of my presentations, and she shares what she learned from it in the section on *"Planting seeds...and pruning weeds at the end of the chapter."*

### *Ranting, Raving and Relationships*

Over the years that I've been working on gender communication issues in business, I've seen numerous women sidetracked by bad advice. The worst bit of it, in my opinion, is this idea that women should "be more like men" in order to get ahead. If a woman's priority is "people first," how can she possibly pretend that she really cares more about "things" or results? Mimicking male behavior does not work, because it is inauthentic for the vast majority of women. In the deep recesses of the male psyche, inauthentic equals danger, and to a man, danger means it's time to fight, flight or freeze—not exactly the best conditions for establishing a healthy business relationship.

Ranel, a manager at an automotive manufacturing company, learned that lesson the hard way. She had come up the ranks under a male boss who constantly yelled when talking to his staff. When she hit middle management, Ranel copied that style and screamed at her employees to get them to follow her lead, all to no avail. When she finally phoned me for a coaching session, she was completely demoralized. "I can't get these guys to come through on a single thing I ask them to do," she complained. "No matter what I say, they don't listen. I pound the table, I get in their faces, I yell—nothing works!"

I started off by explaining to Ranel that all of her ranting and raving caused her male employees to see her as a threat to be eliminated. She would shake her index finger in their faces and stridently announce, "Let me tell you one thing! I'm not putting up with this from you!" Inwardly, a man computes a pronouncement like that as a danger, and somewhere back in the ancient wiring of his brain he's thinking, "Must kill beast!" Or else he feels like a grammar school boy being scolded by his mother. Again, neither reaction sets the stage for a healthy business relationship.

I told Ranel that the first thing she needed to do was to stop the yelling and tone things down—literally. I advised her to lower the tone of her voice instead of resorting to the high-pitch screech that came out of her when she was upset. I also recommended that when talking to her staff, she should deliberately slow her speech down from the rapid-fire cadence of her normal conversations.

We worked on a few other techniques and also discussed many of the issues that impact male and female communication in

148

the workplace (which you've been reading about throughout this book). I'll share some of the techniques we used in the next exercise, called *"Speak up!"* First let me tell you how things worked out for Ranel.

Gradually, as Ranel started implementing some of the concepts we discussed in our coaching sessions, her employees began to respond more positively. One day, she phoned me in tears, and said, "I can't believe it! They're listening to me for the first time! They love me now…it's amazing!"

I know, if someone like Ranel can turn her situation around, anyone can. She didn't give anything up by adapting her management style to communicate with the men she worked. She simply adjusted it and became more effective.

As Ranel's story demonstrates, however, not all women are naturally adept at nurturing workplace relationships. In some cases, women have a harder time communicating with other women than they do with men. You can find out more about this issue in **"Working with Women…"** at the end of the chapter.

Now, let's turn to the exercise that was so helpful to Ranel.

## EXERCISE: Speak Up!

When Ranel began to speak more slowly and in a lower tone of voice, she became much more effective in getting her message across to employees. That's because, when you alter the tone of your voice, you actually change the meaning of what you're saying. As an example, read the sentence "Mary, please close the door" aloud four times— each time placing emphasis on a different word.

- *Mary,* please close the door-—(Mary is singled out.)
- Mary, *please* close the door—(How many times do I have to ask you?)
- Mary, please *close* the door—(Close it completely!)
- Mary, please close *the* door—(Close a particular door— the door and not the window, etc.)
- Mary, please close the *door*—(Close the door; not anything else.)

From this simple example, you can see how a slight change in tone conveys a very different message. Through the tone of their voices, women tend to emphasize relationships, collaboration and consensus building. The reason few women resort to yelling is that doing it could damage relationships, and it certainly does not reflect a collaborative approach. (Plus, let's face it, a man can sometimes get away with raising his voice because he's seen as being passionate or forceful— but if a woman does it, she's more likely to be perceived as being out of control.)

Women may be aware of how their tone of voice enables them to connect to others and convey inclusiveness. But they may not be as conscious of other aspects of their speaking style that can undercut their ability to communicate effectively. In the next sections of this exercise, you'll explore some of these aspects of communication—specifically, how *tonality,* *inflection* and *indirect statements* affect male perceptions of you.

## *Tonality*

Imagine watching two people in a conversation; one is talking loudly and the other very softly. Do you think there's much communication-taking place? Unlikely. You would not have to hear the words to know that something is off. The same thing occurs in business settings. If you don't match the volume of a male, it signals that something is wrong. And because men are looking for strong team members, someone who speaks very softly will be perceived as weak, and not as a good candidate for the team. That assessment is not necessarily true, of course, but remember, perceptions *are* reality to the beholder.

**Volume** is only one part of the overall tonality of your voice that affects your ability to communicate effectively. Your tonality also includes the **pitch, speed** and **cadence** with which you speak. In terms of how these aspects of your tonality are perceived by males, here are a few general observations for you to keep in mind:

- *Pitch:* A high-pitched voice will not be as well received by a man as a lower-pitched one.
- *Speed:* Women tend to speak too fast when talking to men, so slow down. One executive I know purposefully avoids drinking coffee before she goes into high-pressure meetings because she knows it causes her to talk even faster than she normally would.
- *Cadence:* By cadence, I mean how the person transitions between one sentence and another. If a person speaks in a machine-gun "rat-a-tat" cadence, you should also. Conversely, if the transitions are gentle and smooth, then yours should be as well.

When it comes to the tonality of your voice, a good guideline is that you should try to match or come close to the tonality of the other person you're speaking with. If a man is speaking softly, do the same. If he is speaking loudly, you must also. You should also make an effort to come closer to the other person's pitch, speed and cadence as well. Don't make it a contest; just try to alter your tone to come within ten percent of the tonality of the person you're speaking with. Over time, something magical occurs—it becomes hard to tell who is matching whom. You'll both tend to meet somewhere in the middle and begin to feel you're "on the same wavelength." Achieving that rapport is easier when two people share a similar tonality. But when two people are very dissimilar, matching tonality becomes more important. If you don't attempt to align your tonality with the other person, the unconscious message is: "This person is very different from me…" so my choices are to fight (become angry or frustrated), fear ("I had better watch what I say… "), or freeze (ignore, change the subject, glaze over).

You can see by these responses, that paying attention to your tonality can make a big difference in how your words are received.

**Your Turn:**

Over the next several weeks, make a conscious effort to practice matching the tonality of the people you speak with and notice how they respond. Try "mismatching" their tonality as well, and take note of their reactions. Use the space below for your observations.

_____

_____

_____

_____

_____

_____

_____

_____

_____

_____

## *Inflection*

Some women have a tendency to complete a statement by letting their voices drift higher than at the beginning of the sentence, so they end on an upward inflection. The result is that they sound as though they are asking a question even when they are actually issuing a formal directive. Other women may understand that this "question mark" ending to sentences is a command that is delivered nicely. Men do not.

Among males, normal requests and commands are delivered by ending sentences with a downward or flat inflection. Practice that—and also be careful not to emphasize a particular word when you deliver a request, comment or command. For example, the sentence "Please *sit* down" where the word "sit" is emphasized carries less authority that if it is delivered with a simple downward inflection at the end, without any undue emphasis.

## **Your Turn:**

Start noticing how other women end their sentences. Do their voices drift upward even when they're making simple statements? What about men—how do their inflections change? After you've listened to others a bit, start to become aware of your own tendencies. Think back over a situation when you did not feel you got your message across to another person. Was it because your inflection was not consistent with the content of what you were trying to convey? Write your observations here: _____

_____

_____

_____

_____

_____

_____

_____

_____

_____

_____

_____

**TIP:** Ask permission to tape conversation or meeting so that you can hear how you sound to others. Listen to your inflections and how well you match the tonality of others.

### Indirect Statements

Words such as "could," "would," and "perhaps," or statements like "…if it's not too much trouble," or "…I don't want to bother you," can enhance connections with others. Women understand this. Again, men do not.

Men use direct communication. They prefer to command or tell rather than to ask. They also interpret communications literally. When males hear some of the indirect words or statements women tend to use ("…if it's not too much trouble," etc.), they unconsciously interpret the speaker as being weak and unsure of themselves or as someone who does not know what she wants (and who is probably not a good member for the team).

In the first column below, I have listed some common examples of indirect statements. In the second column, I show you how a man might interpret those statements inwardly—even if he doesn't say anything out loud. Then, in the third column, you will see a more effective way of delivering these statements.

| Request | Male's Interpretation | More Effective |
|---|---|---|
| "Could you have this report done today?" | "Yes I could ... *if* I get around to it (... but it doesn't sound important)." | "Please have this report done and on my desk by 4 p.m. today." |
| "I don't want to bother you, but I need to talk with you about..." | "Then why are you bothering me? It, and you, don't seem important." | "I need to talk with you today about ... When is a good time?" |
| "Perhaps it would be better if we did it this way..." | "Perhaps it would— but you don't seem to know, so I'll stick with the way I'm doing it!" | "I appreciate your efforts/input; however, I want you to do it this way." |

**Your Turn:**

In the first column below, write down a common exchange you have experienced or witnessed with men in your workplace. Then write the possible interpretation of your words from the male's perspective (using the second column). See if you can come up with a more effective way of making the statement from column one, and write it in the third column.

| Request | Male's Interpretation | More Effective |
|---|---|---|
|  |  |  |

When Celeste did this exercise, she was amazed to see how easily other people could misperceive her, especially by the men with whom she worked. "Here I thought I was being this powerful businesswoman," she says, "but I was sabotaging myself without even knowing it. I was raised in the south and didn't realize how much I went up on the end of my sentences instead of using a downward inflection. And I will never again issue a direct request with the word 'could' in the sentence!"

As both Celeste and Ranel discovered, they didn't have to completely change their personalities once they walked through the office doors. They simply needed to become more aware of how they sounded and adjust their communication style to get the outcomes they wanted.

Throughout this chapter, you've seen how conflicts can arise because men tend to make relationships a secondary priority. But you've also seen how those conflicts can be resolved through communication. You do not have to sacrifice relationships for results, nor turn yourself into a pale imitation of a man to succeed. You can do it by being true to yourself, playing to your strengths and making simple adjustments to your speaking style so you can be heard.

## *Planting Seeds—and Pruning Weeds*

Bethany is one of the few women to score some successes in the tough world of venture capital investing. She's done it, she says, by slowly developing relationships over time. When she wrote down some of her experiences (as part of the "Rewarding Relationships" exercise), Bethany named her strategy "Planting Seeds."

"Bit by bit," Bethany explains, "I'd plant the seeds for long-term relationships with people that I might not actually do any business with for years. I'd have coffee with them… drop them notes… that sort of thing."

"The men in my field couldn't understand what I was doing," she continues. "They said I was wasting my time. But at one of the main conferences in my area of expertise, I knew every single one of the major presenters, and they all made time to talk with me. That happened because I take the long view and I spend time 'planting seeds'—which I regard as a female approach to relationships."

Bethany's facility at developing relationships, however, does not always bear fruit. "That's when I have to do what I call 'pruning weeds,'" she says. "I have to let go of my hurt feelings when things don't turn out as I expect them to. For instance, I did a huge favor for an old acquaintance from business school and connected him to a number of key contacts. But when he was setting up a panel for an important presentation, he cut me out of it without a second thought. I realized that he was playing the game of "I win, you lose,' while I was looking for a 'win-win.' I felt he 'owed' something to me because of our relationship, but he didn't look at it that way at all."

"Sometimes," Bethany adds, "we women get so focused on nurturing relationships that we forget—not everyone is playing by those same rules."

*Tip:* When you are developing relationships with people, both men and women, you will meet a lot of good people and a few that are not. The guy who didn't return Bethany's favor would most likely fall into the "not-so-good" category—and he would have no hesitation in treating another man as he did Bethany. I have a saying that I use when someone has disappointed me (that is—they didn't act as I had hoped they would):

- **Some will.** (Act in positive manner.)
- **Some won't.**
- **Some waiting.** (There are plenty of other good people waiting to meet you.)
- **So what?** (Who cares about the few "not so goods" in the world? Let them go and move on.)

### Working with Women

Just because females tend to put relationships first and things (or results) second, it does not mean they are necessarily better at managing those relationships than men. At some point in my communication seminars, a few women will invariably raise the issue of problems they've had with other females in the workplace that are different from those that involve males. I normally let the participants talk a little about those issues right then. But this book is not intended to delve too deeply into that aspect of your work life. (I've got my hands full here just trying to explain the male point of view!) Perhaps I'll deal with female-to-female communication issues in a future book. I do, however, want to pass on to you some of the observations other women have shared with me in regards to this issue:

**Jackie,** for instance, works for a high-powered female attorney and says she rarely receives compliments on her work—or even a "Good afternoon," from her boss. "She's not the kind of person you're going to get a 'warm fuzzy' from," Jackie says. "I don't take it personally, and if I do get an acknowledgement, I wear it proudly because they are few and far between."

"I think it's just difficult for her to show appreciation," Jackie adds. "That probably stems from what she's had to do to get where she is today. I think it hardens some women."

**Consuela** always thought it would be easier to work with a woman—until she was assigned to the office of a female vice president in her division. "She was polite," Consuela says, "and she always gave me high marks in my performance reviews—but she didn't trust many people and she just played things very close to the vest. I finally figured out that her attitude was all about her, and it really had nothing to do with me."

**It took all of Carolyn's** ability to be patient and polite when she had to deal with an executive assistant that the other employees referred to as the "prison warden." "She was just very tough, very rude," Carolyn recalls, "and she was fiercely protective of the executive she worked for. So it wasn't too easy to get on his calendar if my boss needed to meet with him."

"Since I was new to the company," Carolyn says, "I realized that I would have to be the one to adapt to her and not the other way around. I made up my mind, though, that I was going to win her over. I was nice to her, but never phony. And I never talked behind her back."

Slowly, Carolyn says, the woman started coming around and being easier to work with. "It probably took me six or seven years, but I never gave up—and I was determined to win. Over the years, I did a few favors for her, and now when she sees me, she always smiles and asks how I'm doing. I knew all along that it was just her personality—and it wasn't me. And I also knew that I was going to have to be the one to go the extra mile."

Carolyn, however, was not as willing to accept the ill treatment dished out by Cassie, a woman in her twenties who Carolyn trained for her administrative duties. "While she was still a temp, she was just wonderful," Carolyn says. "But the minute she became a permanent hire, she did a complete about face. Every time we talked, she would mouth off at me—but I never retaliated."

Then one day, when Carolyn was ready to leave for a long-planned vacation, Cassie informed her that she, herself, was going to take a week off. "I felt like slapping her," Carolyn admitted, "but of course I didn't. I managed to get someone else to cover the work while I was gone and Cassie eventually left the company."

"But now," Carolyn says, "she's come back and is trying to mend fences with people. I have a large network throughout the company and I know she's alienated any number of other staff members. She's really out of place and she steers clear of me—although I am polite when I see her."

When she mentors other women at work, Carolyn points out to them the importance of not burning bridges behind them as Cassie did. "You have to remember," she says, "you're *building* a network of relationships—not tearing one down."

And, she always reminds them of the most time-honored advice about having good relationships: "Just remember." Carolyn says, "What goes around, comes around."

***Author's notes***: From my experience, two of the most frequent causes for friction between female managers and their subordinates are: Women tend to expect that another female will value relationships and empathy the same way as they do. When that doesn't occur, the bond of sisterhood is broken and creates hurt feelings.

The second reason is that many female executives have bought into the notion that to succeed in business they must act like a man. It is a rare woman who can act like a man without feeling inauthentic (and vice versa). This causes tremendous stress, that typically shows up as a cold and perhaps caustic behavior.

## BRAIN: (Appendix)
## Insula

In explaining the function of the insula, *The New York Times* characterized it as: "… the wellspring of social emotions… " Sandra Blakeslee made that observation in her article entitled, "A Small Part of the Brain, and Its Profound Effects" (published February 6, 2007). Blakeslee went on to write that the "...frontal insula is where people sense love and hate, gratitude and resentment, self-confidence and embarrassment, trust and distrust, empathy and contempt, approval and disdain, pride and humiliation, truthfulness and deception, atonement and guilt." Other researchers have noted that the insula is larger and more active in women— and that may explain why females are more likely than men to empathize with others and to emphasize relationships.

# Chapter 7: Be a Sport!

The offsite volunteer project proved to be a hit with everyone. Leann and her co-workers from the marketing department had a great time working together, and they also managed to repair and re-paint a fifth-grade classroom, all in one day.

The young students working on the project also enjoyed the camaraderie. Once the paintbrushes were put away, they suggested a game of kickball pitting the males against the females. Laughter and cheers erupted throughout the game until it dissolved into something of a tie. Leann and the other women assumed the game was over and started saying goodbye to the students. But then, an argument broke out among some of the men from her company who insisted that their team actually scored an additional point—which would have made them the winners.

"The women were over it," Leann recalls, "but the guys couldn't let it go. They wanted a resolution about who really won. It was unreal. We were ready to go home, but the guys kept going back and forth about the game. They were teasing each other... one-upping... all of that... they just *had* to know who the winner was. The bus for the kids finally came and that put an end to it… otherwise I think we might have been there all night!"

Like Leann, you may have a hard time understanding why a group of adult men could spend their time arguing over the results of a schoolyard game of kickball. But the guys were simply doing what they've always done whenever they've stepped onto a playing field: competing for status. As they are growing up, child development experts tell us, boys play mostly competitive games with clear winners and definite losers in order to establish the hierarchy within a group. Girls, by contrast, are more likely to engage in cooperative play where they take turns or play "just for the fun of it," without always declaring a winner.

Naturally, then, Leann and the other women were baffled by the men's insistence on deciding who won the game. And the men—at least those who bothered to give it a second thought—were equally puzzled that the women did NOT care about knowing who won. The views of both the women and the men in this situation underscore the idea that each gender sees the world through its own lenses. Besides recognizing this gender gap in perceptions, you might also understand the behavior of the men from Leann's company a little better if you recall the discussion from Chapter 3, about how important it is for males to know their place in the pack. Don't forget, too, the unwritten rule men live by: "I Win, You Lose, Next Game!™" If there's no clear winner or loser, how can men move on to the "next game"? That's why the guys felt they had to resolve the kickball game one way or the other.

Because games and sports play such a big role in male culture—and sports metaphors are rampant in the business world—it's important to examine these differences between male and female attitudes about these activities. And to discover the roots of those attitudes, we have to look into the forces that shaped the behavior of men and women long ago.

## A Good Hunter: Must Respect the Rules

Humans spent almost one million years as hunters and gatherers before they turned to farming about 10,000 years ago—practically "yesterday" from the anthropologist's point of view. Although agriculture created a relatively abundant food supply, the old memories and instincts for hunting did not fade away. Just because they became farmers, men did not lose the skills they developed as hunters in the *Homo sapiens* era—skills like chasing, running, aiming, throwing and killing, and of moving as one cohesive group in order to bring down a large beast. Instead, those ancient skills were put to different uses, that of controlling and domesticating their prey. The old hunting urges also found other new outlets: games and sports.

Early sports retained many aspects of the ancestral hunt, including chasing and killing live prey. While modern day rodeos still involve catching animals on the run, the actual "killing" is only symbolic in the contemporary sports world.

Interestingly, anthropologists have discovered a link between early man and bronco busters of today. Researchers surmise that in order to kill a large animal, a *H. sapiens* man jumped on the back of the beast while the other hunters would quickly dispatch it—a tactic that could result in many injuries to the rider. In studying those injuries, anthropologists found that they were strikingly similar to those of a particular class of modern athletes: rodeo riders!

Even though they are no longer pursuing large animals, athletes today still enjoy the thrill of the chase and the idea of capturing the "prey" is resolved when one team wins. Our more popular sports, such as football, soccer, basketball, etc., all reflect aspects of ancient hunting: They involve a team (cooperative hunting pack), aiming a weapon (the ball) at a defended goal (the prey). Sports, then, are not merely physical exercises; they actually replicate the work of primeval hunters in chasing down animals and aiming weapons at them. Viewed in this light, perhaps you can begin to appreciate the importance of sports to many males, because they echo that ancient call to hunt and defend territory.

Another aspect of sports can be traced back to the legacy left by *Homo sapiens* hunters: rules. Of necessity, these hunters studied their environment in minute detail and looked for anything that could make it possible for them to survive in it. They had to understand how the animals moved, how they reacted when startled, their seasonal patterns and so on. Through trial and error, they discovered that following certain principles gave them some control over their environment. For instance, if all members of the hunting party ran toward the prey and speared it at the same time, they could bring it down together. But if one of them decided to jump ahead of the rest and throw his spear alone, he might be trampled—and possibly get the rest of them killed as well. So they had to enforce the "rule" that everyone needed to throw their spears at the same time. A good hunter, then, knew he had to respect the rules.

This legacy of rule making can also be seen in research that shows more males than females are systematizers. (See details in the *"Brain Basics"* section of this chapter.) Men, generally, enjoy creating systems. They like finding out how things work and observing the results of their experiments: "If I do this, then *that* happens." Think about the elaborate, step-by-step processes men have developed for everything from building cars to launching rockets to the moon. Look at the male penchant for placing one digit after another to create complex computer codes for software. As systematizers, males recognize that rules provide order, a means for control. And in the case of games, rules give them a way to keep score.

## Bending the Rules

To males, rules are rules and are therefore sacrosanct. At the same time, however, men love to find loopholes around the rules they don't like. How many times have you seen opposing players on the sports field argue about whether a goal should count or not, based on a technicality. Even when referees make their rulings, the players (and spectators) will often continue the argument. You might think men don't like this aspect of the game, given how tempers flare. You would be wrong. Arguing and debating the rules is a necessary and enjoyable part of the game, because they offer an opportunity for gaining status and respect!

What about women? How do they get around the rules they don't like? Simple. They change them. When little girls play together, they tend to set up "win-win" games instead of zero-sum contests where "I win and you lose." In fact, researchers have found that if a game is headed toward one young girl winning at the expense of another, the girls will alter the rules so they all can both be victorious—or else they'll just let the game peter out and move on to another activity.

## Don't Change the Rules

The lesson that you can draw from this research into child's play is that while women may be more comfortable with a work style where they can change the "rules," most men are not.

I pointed out this gender difference to Julia who asked me for advice on how to get a faster response from her boss when she needed him to sign documents so various projects could move ahead. Julia came up with the idea of putting all of the papers into an orange folder and leaving it on his desk with sticky notes telling him where signatures were needed. For a while, her system seemed to be working, but then he began ignoring the folder and Julia was back to square one.

"I don't know what happened," she said during our phone consultation. "I've been putting everything he needs to sign into the folder and we were going along just fine. Then I figured that since I had his attention for the signatures, I'd go ahead and ask him to look over a few other little items, so I started jotting down some quick questions and also put them in the folder."

When Julia told me that, I recognized the problem. By adding the notes into the folder, she changed the "rule." See, her boss looked at that orange folder and knew it meant "sign papers." Once she added her questions to the folder, he viewed it as a change from a quick, simple chore (writing his signature) into a more complex task (thinking about and answering Julia's questions). His response, then, was to put the whole folder aside until he had time to address the questions—that's why Julia's method broke down.

"You confused the guy," I told Julia when I explained how her additional notes represented a rule change to her boss. "If the folder is only for documents that need a signature, make sure that's all you put in it."

"Once you set a rule," I reminded her, "stick with it."

A few weeks later, Julia called me back to report that she had gotten her "orange folder rule" back in place and the system was working smoothly again.

I purposefully used this simple example of what can happen in the workplace because of the differences in the way males and females think about sports and "rules." While the fortunes of Julia's company were not riding on the resolution to her problem, imagine how much energy and effort she and her boss saved by this simple adjustment in her communication— not to mention the potential savings in time it represented to others who were waiting for approval on the documents in the folder.

Now think about how this ordinary, everyday situation can be magnified when it comes to larger issues in your workplace. Suppose a woman executive has to announce a major policy change for the business. Any time employees have to deal with a change, it can be difficult for them. But for the males in her audience, new policies may be even harder to adjust to, because they represent a potential threat to their position in the pack. Plus, they may unconsciously bristle because the "rules" are being changed, and that goes against their fundamental understanding of how the "game" is supposed to be played. In such a situation, it's important to frame the new policy not as a *change* to a rule, but rather as an *exception* to it. For example, the executive could say something like: "Our main objective remains the same—growth and profitability. However due to the current business climate, a modification in how we accomplish the result is needed." This is similar to the addition of "instant replay" to professional football. The rules were not changed; rather a better way of interpreting the rules (whether the player out of bounds or not) was added.

Essentially, rather than changing a rule outright it is much better to keep it in place and find loopholes to it. A common example in today's challenging times is the annual director's meeting. Suppose the "rule" has been that the directors go to Cancun for a week to plan for the upcoming year. This has been standard practice for 20 years. Now, due to declining revenues, the CEO has decided to hold the meeting at the company's headquarters in Peoria. Note that the CEO has demonstrated the rule is the rule: "We must have a meeting." And he also explains the exception to the rule: "Due to the downturn, however, we will have the meeting in Peoria."

To women this seems trivial and is just spin. In many ways it is. Bear in mind that men have much stronger and unconscious need for adherence to rules than do women. Why fight it? Just find an exception or loophole to the rule rather than declaring the rule null and void. You get what you want with a lot less hassle. Another benefit is that men love finding exceptions to the rule, and they will jump to your aid in helping you find it.

How many times have you watched men argue whether someone is out of bounds? They are not arguing about the rule; a *player is out* if his foot is out of bounds when the ball is caught, they are arguing whether the foot was out of bounds!)

### Sports Talk

Walk into any typical office in the United States and sooner or later, you're bound to hear talk about sports—either a local team, a national sensation, or even imaginary athletic contests. As Lucinda shared in one of my workshops: "Everything in my office revolves around sports. If the men aren't talking about the last big game, they're talking about the next one. And if that's not enough, then they start talking about their fantasy leagues! Who can keep up with all of that?"

While sports banter may seem a harmless recreation, it can also have career consequences for some women. "I've found it's harder to have real rapport with my supervisor because I'm not that interested in the same sports he is," Nina says. "He seems to bond easily with the men in my department, because, when it comes to sports, they talk his language and I don't. That makes it a little more difficult for us to work together." (Abby, too, found that sports talk blocked her path when she tried to close a deal, and you can read her story in the section entitled *"Bonding, Baseball and Business"* at the end of the chapter.)

In developing communication strategies with Nina and Lucinda, the first thing I pointed out to them was that they did not have to pretend to be super fans, but they could make an effort to join in the conversations about sports. I suggested that they could skim the sports pages or listen to a few minutes of talk radio during their commute time so they would be clued in a little better to what was happening in the world of athletics. They didn't have to deliver a play-by-play description of a championship game, but when workplace talk turned to sports, they could throw in a few questions or comments to show they were listening and interested. I know some women may not like this idea that *they* have to be the ones to make the effort to adjust to male-dominated sports talk. But remember, this book is about helping you to be **more effective** in your communication at work and to find ways of reducing the stress in your interactions with men at the office.

After following my advice for a few weeks, Nina reported that work with her supervisor was going more smoothly. "It has made a difference to show a little more interest in football," Nina says, "even though I like basketball better." I also looked for other areas where I could connect with my boss and some of the other males at the office. I love movies, and it turns out they love movies too. You may not be able to bond with the guys over everything, but you can usually find some place where you share some common ground and go from there."

Women aren't the only ones who need to adjust, either. Helen, an Executive Administrator for the CEO of a Fortune 500 company relayed this story to me: Walter, the CEO, is an avid golfer. Every year he invites his senior staff to a golf getaway. Naturally everyone goes. Do all the men share Walter's passion for golf? Hardly. Helen says that at least a third of them would rather walk across hot coals than to spend hours on a golf course. Why do they do it? Well the obvious answer would be that they want to keep their jobs. But that is not the real reason. These men (and women) are key members of the company who are very talented, so missing the golf game would hardly be considered reasons for firing them. No, the real reason they go is that participating in the game (the primordial hunt) provides an invaluable way to bond and increase their status. It will however, raise a red flag to the rest of the members. They will begin to wonder if he is really committed to the team. If it continues, they will probably get rid of him.

### Men of Action

Another feature of the sports world that shows up in the workplace is this: Men like to see action.

The unspoken code among males is that doing something about a problem is better than doing nothing. And males—as pointed out in the discussion on risk-taking in Chapter 4—get points just for trying to take action, whether they succeed or not.

While men can certainly do their share of procrastinating and passing off responsibility to other people, they nevertheless prefer to be perceived as "men of action." They judge other men by that criterion as well. Because the ever-present struggle for status always lurks in the background of male interactions, men are aware of what happens when they are not seen as being action-oriented. If a man seems to be waiting around for someone else to do something for him, other males interpret that stance as weakness. As a consequence, the weaker male will either be shunned or pushed aside by the stronger ones. In other words, he will not be seen a good team member.

When men ask for help, there is always an unconscious fear that by doing so they will lose status with other males. (Now you know the real reason men won't stop to ask for directions!)

To guard against this loss of status, they take great pains to **let others know what they have done** about a problem or a project, informing their listeners that they stepped forward into the unknown, risking life and limb to find a solution. They do this **before asking for help.**

Of course, the kinds of solutions most men need to find in an ordinary business day may not require them to risk their lives. But whether they are dealing with a paper jam or a tough client, men will still make a point of communicating that they are "men of action."

The important thing for you to notice about this predominantly male characteristic is that men will explain what actions they have taken *before* seeking assistance from others. Let me give you a simple example. I was having a problem with my computer and decided to call Tom, a computer whiz for help. The conversation went something like this:

*Mike:* "Tom, I'm having a problem with my Excel spreadsheet. It wouldn't let me select more than one row at a time so I can move several of them together or delete them. I tried reinstalling Excel, did a virus scan and rebooted the computer." *(Notice how many actions I reported—reinstalling the program, doing a virus scan and rebooting the computer.)*

*Tom:* "Hum…Have you gone online to see if anyone else is seeing this?"

*Mike:* "Yes, several times" *(Implied message: I have really worked on this!)*

*Tom:* "What about Microsoft forum"

*Mike:*  "Yup, nothing…" *(Again: I've already tried taking action.)*

*Tom:*  "Mmm… have you tried restarting the computer to the earlier setting where it did work?"

*Mike:*  "No, I haven't. I am not very familiar with doing that. *(Implied message: I am familiar, just not **very** familiar with it.)* Could you walk me through it?"

*Tom:*  "Sure. Power down again and I'll tell you what to do from there…."

Had I just asked Tom to help without any explanation, he probably would have quizzed me about what I had already tried. If I had told him that I hadn't tried anything, my standing with him would have dropped several notches. Men are expected to "take the bull by the horns" first before turning to anyone else for help.

### Act Before Asking

Why should it matter to you that Tom would have lowered his opinion of me if I hadn't tried to solve my problem before calling him? *Because men will judge you just as they judge other men*—and you will be perceived as weak, less reliable, and worse, less worthy of respect, if you do not take action steps on your own behalf before turning to others.

When asking for advice or help from a man, then, be sure to preface your request by mentioning or enumerating the things you have already done to address the issue, as I did with Tom.

The "rule" for you to remember is this: **Act before asking!**

To see exactly how this rule applies, I want to give you a more in-depth view of it through some real-life examples. In these situations, condensed from the experiences of my friend Steve, an executive coach, you'll see how men follow the rule about taking action before asking for help.

## The Plot:

Steve, an executive coach, has a client, Jerry, who is negotiating an agreement to buy out a partner whose actions have put the company in financial jeopardy. Jerry's attorney wants him to fire the partner "for cause," but Jerry is reluctant to do that. The attorney has drawn up an agreement and advised Jerry to give the partner an ultimatum to sign it or risk being terminated. Jerry told the attorney he'd do so, and is meeting with Steve to discuss the problem.

## Scene 1: "I tried."
*... in which Jerry asks for help without having taken any action himself.*

*Jerry:* "Thanks for coming by on such short notice."

*Steve:* "No problem. What's up?"

*Jerry:* "I want to talk to you about the Buyout Agreement with my partner."

*Steve:* "OK. How's it going? The last time we talked, you were going to give him the documents to sign. Has he done that yet?"

*Jerry:* "That's what I wanted to talk to you about. I tried, but it's not going well..."

*Steve:* "But you gave him the paperwork over a month ago. I thought you agreed with your attorney that he had one week to sign it or else!"

*Jerry:* "Well, I gave it to him after we spoke and he hasn't gotten back to me since then. What do you think I should do?"

*Steve:* "Hmmm…"

You probably don't have to think too hard about what Jerry needs to do in this situation. Obviously, he has to follow up with the partner by phone, email or in person and attempt to move the negotiations forward instead of waiting around for someone else to do it. But this scene gives a clear example of how ineffectual Jerry appears to be, because he has not even taken the most rudimentary action steps to help himself. Steve may decide to assist him—but it will not be without reservations, because he sees Jerry as weak and not likely to heed any of his advice.

## Scene 2: "Look, I did something."
### *… in which Jerry takes some action*

Now let's re-visit the scene and pick it up at the point where Steve reminds Jerry that he gave the partner the paperwork more than a month before.

*Steve:* "…I thought you agreed with your attorney that he had one week to sign it or else!"

*Jerry:* "Yes, I know. But he seemed to be dragging his feet, so I met with him on three separate occasions to discuss any issues he had. *(Implied message: See, I took action.)* I thought it was settled. I even reminded him he caused the problem. I told him he put the company in serious jeopardy and that I had grounds to terminate him for cause!" *(Look, I did something. I told him all the things he did wrong. I really did take action.)*

Steve: "So what happened when you began termination procedures?"

Jerry: "That's why I called you. We had a very contentious meeting when I told him I was starting the termination 'for cause.' He hired an attorney and threatened legal action. I was hoping you had some ideas."

Steve: "Hmmm…"

Jerry has taken action. He met with the partner and talked to him about the issues. He also threatened legal action as originally agreed, at which time the battle escalated. Now he needs Steve's help.

From Steve's point of view Jerry is taking action and is now in need of more counsel. Because Jerry acted on his advice, Steve is confident that he will continue to do so.

The lesson for you, to repeat the "rule" I outlined earlier, is this: Act before asking—*and* let the other person know what you have done.

Especially when you are interacting with males, be sure to first state what you have done to try to solve the problem and let them know you are stumped. Everyone is at some point, and we all know it.

Because men view life as a competition for status and winning they are constantly looking for signs of a strong, action-oriented player who can help them (and their team) win. By adapting to this male "rule" to "act before asking," you will signal that you are someone who can be counted on to take action and to get help appropriately when it's needed.

This next exercise will help you look at ways you can sharpen your orientation to action—and avoid some of the mistakes Jerry made in the first example of his communication with Steve.

## EXERCISE: Women of Action

*Instructions:* In this exercise, you will be looking at your own behavior in terms of "acting before asking." Think back over your work life and use the space below (or other paper to answer the following questions:

Think of an instance in the past when you asked for help from a man without first letting him know what actions you had already taken to solve the problem?

**What** was his response? _____

_____

_____

_____

_____

_____

_____

**How** could you have rephrased that same request?

_____

_____

_____

_____

_____

_____

_____

**Bonus question:** How would another woman have reacted to your request? Why? _____

_____

_____

_____

_____

_____

_____

**Example *(of answers to the first three questions)*:**

*She:*　"I'm having a problem with getting Mary to arrive on time. Do you have any suggestions?"

*He:*　"Sure. Have her see me." *(Implied message: Obviously you can't do it, so I will.)*

In this example, the woman has unconsciously signaled that she can't handle the problem since she has not even tried to do anything about it. The man, in turn, interprets her question as a request to take over.

Let's look at what happens when this same request is rephrased:

*She:* "I'm having a problem with getting Mary to arrive on time. I've warned her several times and finally wrote her up. It still doesn't seem to make a difference. Before I take more drastic action, I wanted to know if you had any experience with this and how I might handle it. Do you have any suggestions? *(Implied message: This time, the woman signals confidence and an action orientation. Clearly, she is asking for his assistance—not for him to take over, because she uses this forceful phrase: "... before **I take** more drastic action...")*

*He:* "Sure, let me give you a few ideas that have worked for me. I'm sure you'll have no trouble implementing them." *(Implied message: Because you are a woman of action, I know you'll follow through on what needs to be done. You're someone I can work with and would like to have on my team.)*

**Your Turn:**

**Can** you think of an instance in the past when you asked for help from a man without first letting him know what actions you had already taken to solve the problem?

_____

_____

_____

_____

_____

_____

_____

_____

_____

**What** was his response?

_____

_____

_____

_____

_____

_____

**How** could you have rephrased that same request?

_____

_____

_____

_____

_____

_____

**Bonus question:** How would another woman have reacted to your request? Why?

_____

_____

_____

_____

_____

_____

After completing this exercise, you should have a clearer picture of three benefits of "acting before asking"

**First,** you help the other person you are communicating with by providing more information on the situation you're trying to resolve.

**Second,** you're paying the other person a compliment—because you are showing that you have worked on the problem without success but you believe he or she can help you.

**Third,** in recounting your efforts, you are giving yourself a personal reminder of your own competence (because you have taken action instead of passively expecting to be "rescued").

As you continue to improve your communication skills using some of the ideas from this chapter—respecting the "rules," adapting to sports talk, and acting before asking—your ability to work with both men and women will also improve. You'll not only "be a sport…" you'll be the one standing in the winner's circle!

## BRAIN BASICS:
### Systemizing vs. Empathizing Brains

The male preference for creating systems and rules seems to spring from their "systemizing" brains, according to Simon Baron-Cohen, a Cambridge professor, who is the author of *The Essential Difference: The Truth About the Male and Female Brain.* "A systematizer," Baron-Cohen has said, "is somebody whose style of thinking is predominantly in terms of understanding things according to rules or laws. You can think of lots of different kinds of systems: mathematical systems (algebra, computer programs), or mechanical systems (computers or cars); natural systems (weather, geology); and social systems (businesses or the military). In each case, when you systemize what you do, you try to understand the system in terms of the laws that govern the system." By contrast, empathizers excel at relationships and at understanding how someone else might feel (and they also want to alleviate that person's distress.) Baron-Cohen has generated a questionnaire to help people rate themselves along the systemizing-empathizing continuum. Based on the results of thousands of these tests, Baron-Cohen estimates that 53 percent of men have systemizing brains, 17 percent have empathizing brains and 24 percent are roughly balanced. (The remaining 6 percent have an "extreme male brain," and these men, according to his theory, demonstrate behavior that may be considered autistic.) He also estimates that 44 percent of women have empathizing brains, 17 percent have systemizing brains, 35 percent have brains that are somewhat balanced between the two poles, and 4 percent exhibit an "extreme female brain" type.

## Bonding, Baseball and Business

Abby was working hard to secure venture capital money for a new company and, during a business reception; she sat down for drinks with one of the key potential investors. One of the men from her company was also at the reception, and he managed to join in on the conversation. "The two guys started talking," Abby recalls, "and the next thing you know, they're bonding over going to Yankee Stadium with their dads when they were six years old. That's the moment the chemistry happened. I watched it—and I got cut out of the deal." While Abby certainly didn't like the outcome of the evening, she chalked it up to experience. "Bonding over sports is just something that I'm not going to do very well. But at the end of the day, I have to realize that there are other things that I do well and I have to capitalize on them. I have my fair share of moments when I *do* connect with other people and I can't dwell on the times I don't."

## Unsportsmanlike Conduct

Candace had been a star basketball player in high school, but she rarely played the game after she earned her MBA and went to work. One day at a company retreat, however, some of her co-workers started shooting hoops and asked Candace to join them in a game. "I didn't even have my real basketball shoes on," Candace remembers. "But it seemed like fun, so I played. Then, my vice-president at the time announced that he was going to guard me." Even though Candace was rusty, her old skills kicked in and she started running circles around him. "I wasn't really trying that hard," she says, "but I was having a really good game and making all kinds of shots." When her team won, the executive was definitely cool toward her. "It wasn't anything overt," Candace says, "but after that game, I felt like he didn't like me anymore… like maybe he was thinking 'I let this girl show me up.' " Looking back on the incident, Candace realized that her moments of glory on the court were not worth the damper it put on her work environment. "If I had to do it over again," she says, "I probably would have eased up a little during the game—because I think it did impact my relationship with that vice president."

Candace learned a valuable lesson about male culture: Don't humiliate your opponent. He may be your teammate tomorrow, or you may have to play him again another day. Of course, there are exceptions. Some men do like to grind down their opponents. For the most part, males understand that it's important for the other guy to save face. If you crush other players, they will either not engage with you or else they will spend an inordinate amount of energy trying to crush you back, rather than playing a good, honest game. Remember, men love the game! And one more thing: If a male gets angry or aloof because you beat him fair and square, you can bet he has a poor self image. Men with a good self image will give a better opponent (women included) high points for a great game. I hear countless stories from men who admire a woman who has a particular skill—because she's someone they want on their team.

## Chapter 8: If You're Going to Run Away, We Won't Let You Play

Angie knew the job would be hard. But she didn't expect the rudeness and outright hostility she heard in the voices of the men she called to seek funding for her new company.

Some of them wouldn't return her phone calls. Others left voice mails laced with expletives, telling her "You're going to fail!" and "You don't know what you're doing!"

Jake, one of her likeliest potential investors, told her to stop sending him emails and declared, "There's no way I'm going to write you a check!"

The negative reception only spurred Angie to work harder. Through sheer dogged persistence, she reached her goal of securing more than $3 million in start-up funds.

Jake, ultimately, did write a check and, surprisingly, became one of Angie's strongest supporters and advisors.

As their relationship strengthened, Angie asked him why he had been so rude during her fund-raising phase. With characteristic bluntness, Jake gave her an answer that women need to hear if they hope to be successful competitors and co-workers with men in business.

"I was harsh with you because I had to make sure you wouldn't run away when things get tough," Jake told her. "I don't want to work with someone or support someone who's going to drop out if times are hard. This is what we (men) do to each other. It's a process you have to go through."

### *Occupational Hazard Warning: Hazing Ahead*
Looking back on the experience, Angie refers to it as her "hazing," an initiation rite she had to endure in order to be accepted as a full-fledged member of the team of men who were among her initial financial backers. "I had to earn their respect," she says now, "I realized that the norms that exist

for men are really strange for us as women. Unless a woman has been through the military or played sports, she's probably not familiar with this hazing behavior that men consider normal."

Angie's experience may sound abusive to you—and, as I've stated previously, you should never accept abuse. At the same time, however, you cannot overlook the lesson in her story because it is a valuable one. **In working with men, you will be tested.** You will be challenged. These behaviors are not personally aimed at you, because, as Jake said to Angie, **that's what men do to each other** (See Ellen's story for another example in *"They'll eat you alive!"at the end of the chapter*).

Remember, men want to be on a winning team and they only want teammates who will help them win. In the rough and tumble game of business, things will go wrong, problems are inevitable and failure is common. The men want to know that their team will stick together when the going is rough. If you're perceived as someone who will fold at the first sign of trouble, they won't let you onto the team. They want members who, in the heat of battle or the hunt, will "watch their back!"

Or, as I say when explaining this male dynamic to women in my seminars: *If you're going to run away, we won't let you play.* Men don't let other "weak" men on the team either (if they can help it), and they're not going to make exceptions for you just because you're female.

Constance, like Angie, has been through a business "hazing" with high-level executives and lived to tell the tale. Her strategy for dealing with this aspect of male behavior is to do extra preparation and background research before she meets someone new or goes into meetings where she is unfamiliar with the other participants.

"Some men present themselves as being very aggressive," Constance says. "They may appear to be very stern, very challenging or very raunchy when meeting someone new. Usually they do that because of old habits that they've carried over from past situations where they used those tactics to establish territory or dominance. That can be very off-putting and throw cold water on a new business relationship—unless you're prepared for their communication style and can look past the male's 'brilliant display of feathers,' so to speak, to find out what the rooster is actually thinking."

"The worst mistake you can make," she points out, "is to not know anything about the person before you walk into an important sales presentation or budget meeting. You have to know what you're getting into, because there can be a big difference between how someone 'postures' in presenting himself and what his actual perspective is."

"Unfortunately," she adds, "you can only get to know his real view over time… and sometimes it's too late if your first meeting goes badly. It's a thousand percent better if you can talk to some people in advance to find out what a man is like, so you can be prepared for any eccentricities."

Just remember, whatever happens: It's not personal. The guy could simply be testing you, or he might be having a bad day, or he could have any number of other reasons for acting as he does, none of which have anything to do with you!

Posturing for position, establishing territory, forcing a colleague through a gauntlet of challenges—all of these behaviors by today's businessmen in their suits and ties, could have just as easily been the actions of cavemen dressed in animal skins. Let's look, for a final time, at how the code of the ancient hunter was passed down through millennia to land in your workplace.

### A Good Hunter: Must be Able to Make Certain the Hunting Party is Victorious

While the women of ancient *Homo sapiens* society formed relationships with each other around nurturing children, the men joined forces to fight physical dangers. They had to work together in groups because their prey was big, fast and deadly. If they didn't back each other up, a dangerous animal could destroy them all. Armed with only primitive spears or rocks, the *H. sapiens* hunters would try to distance themselves from that danger. But they needed to move in relatively closely to their prey to take it down, which meant they had to be able to stand their ground while a huge beast charged at them. Anyone who would cut and run threatened the survival of everyone else in the hunting party. It's no wonder then, that complex testing rituals evolved among males, traces of which can be seen in coming-of-age ceremonies in indigenous societies and the hazing conducted by modern fraternities and gangs. By showing he was able to stay up all night or endure pain, a young male could prove he was tough enough for the rigors of the hunt—just as Angie showed Jake that she could run a company because she withstood the boorish behavior of the investors she contacted.

While the *H. sapiens* males did try to distinguish themselves individually—because the best hunters got the biggest rewards—ultimately, they knew that their lives depended on how well the hunting party worked together as a team. They had to be sure their hunting party was victorious, just as men in corporations today want to ensure that their teams win. And just as his forefathers weeded out less capable or lower status males from the hunt, modern men also keep others off their teams who are not seen as vital contributors.

So how do you position yourself to be considered a valuable addition to teams at work? How do you break into the "boy's club" and get chosen for it? This next section, and those that follow, will give you some insights and ideas to help answer those questions.

### Male Bonding: Why They Exclude You

Imagine growing up with a close group of friends. You run and play together. You're inseparable. In times of stress and pain, you're always there, listening, sympathizing and consoling. You are so close that it seems you can read each other's minds.

As you get a little older, someone suggests you all take up singing as a group. Everyone, except you, can sing. While the others offer support, you know in your heart that you cannot sing. No matter how hard you try, you cannot hold a note.

As time passes, the group is still friendly with you, inviting you to their singing engagements. But it's just not the same. Their lives revolve completely around their singing careers. You don't belong to the group as you once did and everyone knows it. They're on the road most of the time. When they aren't, they're in the studio practicing or recording. You feel really alone for the first time. Now what do you do? You love the group and they love you, but you're not a singer and not really part of them anymore. What would you do in such a situation?

Most likely you would slowly fade away from that group and begin finding new friends who like the same things you do. You'd see your old friends now and again, and when you do get together, it's like old times. The love and friendship is still there during those moments. Yet things can never go back to the way they were. You all have different lives. Now you spend your time with your new friends, the ones with whom you have things in common. This new circle of friends are into basketball, something that you're reasonably good at. You enjoy spending time on the court and the camaraderie that accompanies it. And so life goes on.

You may be wondering what this story has to do with men and women communicating at work, and what role male bonding plays in that dynamic. Let me explain:

The journey I've been describing is the one that all men must travel from the time they are about four to six years old. It is at this age that little boys begin to realize they are different from the "friends" they have been so close with—that is, they come to understand they are different from their mothers and other females. Unlike their mothers, boys know they can never bear a child. They can no longer be part of the "group." So they must begin looking for others who **are** like them— they must turn to other males.

Little girls do not have to make that wrenching journey at such an early age. They can identify with their mothers because, physically, they have the same characteristics. Assuming their bodies are normally healthy, girls can grow up into women who can bear children. The girl has an identity; she is a woman and a giver of life.

Men, by contrast, do not have their identities handed to them. They must *find* their identities by being different from their mothers, from women.

According to Karen Horney, Ph.D., an early pioneer in childhood development, this difference in male and female development is the difference between "being" and "doing." She terms female identity as something that is *ascribed*, while male identity has to be *achieved*. Women are women because of *what they are*; men are men because of *what they do*. A woman's identity as a woman is grounded in the simple fact that she can have children. A man's identity is based upon his continually proving his difference *from* his mother and from other women—and continually proving himself *to* other men.

When they are between four and six years of age, little boys, then, will begin to seek out other males with whom to bond. Their identity is formed from these bonds. They learn to compete and seek status in their male groups. These bonds are strong, lasting and very different from those enjoyed by women. (The difference in bonding patterns between men and women is also reflected in the brain chemistry of each gender. Men, it turns out, secrete less oxytocin, the brain chemical associated with primary bonding (See the *"Brain Basics"* section at the end of the chapter).

While men are constantly competing for status and dominance within the group, the group itself is supreme. Ultimately, the group as a whole must be strong enough to protect all its members from harm. While status is very important, everyone must be willing and able to defend the group in times of danger. Everyone, therefore, is important and must be counted upon to keep the whole unit strong. Sometimes, you have to "take one for the team."

These are primal forces at work. Men understand them and appreciate them—although few could really explain how those forces affect their lives. These bonds are strong and very deep. It is not unusual to hear of men who have risked death to protect the life of another. This happens all the time in war. The bonds formed then are the strongest and most lasting of any on earth. I would even venture to say that these ties are probably stronger and more enduring than those between women. Even as I write this paragraph, the right words to describe it escape me.

The need for male camaraderie lasts a lifetime. In both their professional and personal lives, men need to get together with other men—without the women being around. It's not so much about forming an "old boys club" to keep women out, as it is that men have a need to bond with other men. I am here to tell you that 99 percent of the time this "males-only" bonding time is not about the men getting together and strategizing about how to keep women from advancing.

Granted—some men do purposely do this, but the majority do not. And those men who do this to women will also do the same to another man. As I continue to repeat: It's not personal!

Let's get to the heart of the issue: The problem for women in the workplace is that during these male-bonding sessions, many important business issues get discussed.

If a woman is not present at one of those sessions, she can be in the dark about important decisions the men reach without her. She has to play catch-up once she discovers that a decision has been made. What can she do?

I have two comments about this dilemma:

**First,** there will be times when men will want to be alone without women. These are occasions when men just want to go out and have a good time, share a beer or two, talk about women and sex, etc. Forget about these sessions. Trust me; you wouldn't want to be there even if they invited you. Go out and relax with your female friends.

**Second,** there are other occasions when business problems *are* discussed and corrective actions are suggested. *These are the times when you do need to be present.* These bonding times for the men will tend to revolve around sports or some competitive activity such as golf, football, fishing, softball, etc. You don't have to be good at these activities. Remember, men give big points to people who show up and try. And you don't have to like these sports either. I can tell you from experience that many of the men who are showing up don't really enjoy them either. *But you do need to be there.*

## *"Making the Team"*

How do you go about getting invited to "join the team"? Here are a few suggestions that may help you:

1. Want to be included in a group meeting or activity? Just ask! Simple as it sounds, it's probably the most effective tactic you can use. Men generally don't beat around bush when they want something. They tend to be very direct and so should you. If you don't ask, men will assume you are not interested. If you know that several men play golf together, ask if you can join

them the next time they go out to the course. If you don't play golf, and you know important issues are being discussed on the course, take some lessons and get out there. That's what other men do.

2. Form your own group and invite the men either to join you or compete with you. Keep it light and fun. Challenge them. They will love it.

3. Arrange an outing to a game or sporting event and invite key people (both men and women) to attend.

4. Enlist the help of a mentor or advocate. Men do this all the time. They will ask other men to help introduce them to a group or organization. I once asked a friend to get me an invitation to an exclusive men's group where membership is only by invitation. He was glad to do it. I then had to introduce myself to other members. Eventually, after six months, I was asked if I would like to join, and I did. Fortunately, in most business settings, getting into the group does not take that long. But if it does take a while—and it's worth it to you—then do it. Don't get discouraged; sometimes it just takes time.

5. Whatever you do, do not take anything personally— because it's not personal!

**If you're still excluded:**
What happens if, for some reason, you find that decisions and policies that affect you and your job are being crafted without your input? Or suppose you've asked to be invited to meetings where strategies are discussed, but you never get

the invitation. Then it is appropriate and necessary for you to be very blunt and direct. You will need to be assertive—not aggressive—in your communication. Here's an example:

*You:* "May I share a concern that I have with you?" *(Pause until he answers.)*

*John:* "Sure. What's up?"

*You:* "I know that you, Tim and Mike played golf last week and discussed the Acme account. And you made some decisions that have repercussions on my group."

*John:* "Yeah... I was meaning to talk to you about that..."

*You:* "I can understand that you probably didn't mean to do, it but it does have a major impact on my group. I have to admit that I'm a bit angry, as this is not the first time this has happened. I want to do a good job but I can't if I'm not involved in the decision-making process."

*John:* "Hmmm..."

*You:* "I need to be included in the process from the beginning—not at the tail end of things. How can we make that happen?"

*John:* "Well how about if we all go for coffee on Thursday..."

## Six Steps for Assertive Communication

As mentioned above, when you are speaking directly to someone about a touchy issue, it is important for you to be assertive rather than aggressive. This six-part script will show you how to strike the right balance:

1. **Event:**
   - ***When you...*** (Describe what happened. Your description must be factual, not conjecture.)
2. **Impact:**
   - ***I felt...***
   - (Describe your feelings, whether frustrated, angry, upset, etc.)
3. **Reason:**
   - ***Because...***
   - (Explain why you felt as you did.)
4. **Request:**
   - ***I request... (or, I prefer, want, would like, etc.)***
   - (Describe the corrective action you want.)
5. **Outcome:**
   - ***That way, (the result, outcome, etc.) will be...***
   - (Describe the benefit of the corrective action to the other person.)
6. **Agreement:**
   - ***Will you do that?... Is that fair?... Are we in agreement...? How can we make that happen?)***
   - (Confirm the corrective action.

## Example:

***When you*** *gave me only two hours to complete the Jefferson report,* ***I felt*** *frustrated,* ***because*** *it did not give me enough time to proofread it thoroughly. In the future,* ***I request*** *that you give me at least four hours on a report this size.* ***That way,*** *I will be able to make sure that everything is correct and am able to do the very best job for you.* ***How can we make that happen?***

Things to remember when being assertive:

- You are delivering this message because it is in the **best interest** of both parties.
- Tonality is key. Any sign of sarcasm, anger or hostility will neutralize it. Speak as though your request is the right thing to do: After all, it is!
- Include all six steps of the script. Resist the temptation to leave something out because it is too uncomfortable to mention.
- Memorize the script, then deliver it in your words—but remember to include all six parts.
- Both men and women will love it when you are straightforward and assertive rather than being aggressive.

While it takes some effort on your part to become part of the team, the good news is that when you're accepted to the roster, your work burdens become lighter. "Once you're in, you're in," says Cindy, a sales manager. "When you're brought into the inner circle and become more aware of what's going on, everything changes. Your job gets easier and you're much happier!"

### *Running the Obstacle Course to Make the Team*

Let's take a moment to recap here. You've seen how male "hazing" in business can be one obstacle to your success. And you've learned a little about how to deal with the type of male bonding behavior that can also stand in your way.

Now I'd like to turn your attention to a few other roadblocks to your making the team—two of which may be set up by men. These are behaviors I call the "kid-glove treatment" and the "incredible invisible woman syndrome." Then we'll move on to look at a roadblock that *you* may be setting up yourself—it's a signal that women unwittingly send that shows they may not be the best pick for a winning team.

### The Kid-Glove Treatment

While business "hazing" can be tough enough to overcome, at least the obnoxious comments are out in the open. Women face a more difficult challenge, however, when they have to deal with a practice that is the opposite of hazing: *the kid-glove treatment.*

This type of treatment often comes from men who may be understandably confused about how to communicate with women without hurting their feelings—or who may be worried about ending up on the losing end of a harassment suit. Regardless of the motivation behind it, when a woman is treated with kid gloves, she is automatically relegated to a "one-down" position of weakness. Whether benign or not, the kid-glove treatment can be damaging to a woman's business success.

Frances got a front-row view of this problem when she attended a roundtable discussion with a group of entrepreneurs. When Sharon, a consultant, rose to make her presentation, she told the group that she wanted to grow her company by 40 percent—but only three of her seven employees could produce work that was billable to clients.

"It was obvious to me that her business model couldn't work," Frances says. "Everyone looked at each other but no one said a thing. I finally spoke up and asked her a simple question: 'What about this model do you think will create profitability?' Sharon kind of talked around it, but she never really answered the question. All the rest of the group was somewhat quiet and kind of staring at me. So I finally asked 'What do you guys think?' A couple of the men made some mild comments about the fact that maybe there was too little profit on the bottom, but that was it."

"And then," Frances adds, "everyone applauded and told her it was a good presentation!"

By contrast, when the group listened to the next presenter after Sharon, a man who was expanding his delivery business, they strongly questioned everything he said about his plans for the company.

"We spent an hour ripping apart all of his assumptions," Frances recalls. "We tore him up and asked him all kinds of questions. He took it and sometimes even laughed along with the rest of us. Everyone was very engaged."

"No one gave Sharon anywhere near the level of feedback that we gave that guy," she adds. "We women sort of get the short end of the stick because everyone is worried about us bursting into tears or having our feelings hurt."

Jacqueline, too, has discovered the downside of being treated like a porcelain doll. "One of my pet peeves," Jacqueline says, "is dealing with men who behave in an overly-courtly, overly-complimentary way. That's often an insidious signal that they expect the woman to behave in an overly-compliant way."

"This behavior always worries me," she adds, "because it's often a subtle form of warning: 'I will treat you nicely as long as you know your place and stay in it.' "

As Jacqueline points out, the "kid-glove treatment" can be subtle. And since it can vary in individual situations, there is no one-size-fits-all answer for it.

Men may offer the benign form of this treatment, because they are legitimately concerned that a woman may start crying and/or never let it go if they are too blunt with their assessments or managerial directions. While men may be able to handle confrontations with other men, most males are profoundly uncomfortable in the face of a woman's tears.

From what I've seen, Jacqueline's experience is somewhat rare, because not many men are inclined to be "nice" as long as the woman "knows her place." More commonly, men are afraid that if they say what's on their minds—as they would to another male—the woman won't be able to take it. (I can tell you that most men would rather have their fingernails pulled out rather than face a woman who might cry. We don't know how to deal with it. We feel powerless, which is not a good place for a male.)

By managing your emotions in the workplace and speaking forthrightly, you will earn a reputation as someone who does not need the kid-glove treatment, so you will probably not be subject to it. You can also build relationships with mentors and ask them for honest feedback about your work or business proposals (to avoid the fate of Sharon who did not get helpful information from the business group when she made her presentation.)

On the other hand, if a male is actually using the "over-courteous" approach to put you a step down or "keep you in your place," you will need to use your own savvy and sense of humor to disarm the situation. In the face of someone who does not treat you as a competent business equal, you can call on several skills you've learned in this book (see "Exceptional You!" exercise in chapter 5 and recall your strengths.

Avoid upward inflections in your conversation unless you are asking a question and check to see if you're matching the volume level and cadence of males you interact with as explained in the "Speak Up" exercise of Chapter 6. Cadence, you may recall, refers to the way a person ends one sentence and begins another. Some people will end a sentence abruptly and immediately begin another in a staccato fashion. Other people transition from one sentence to another in a soft, flowing manner. By matching the other person's tonality, you put yourself on equal ground with them, instead of being "one down."

And always, always remember: it's not personal. If a guy feels the need to put you down a peg by using the kid-glove treatment, it means he's insecure about himself—and it's not about you!

## The Incredible Invisible Woman

Of all the questions women ask in my workshops, one comes up time and again—and it seems to be the one that causes women the most aggravation. The question goes like this:

"Why is it that *I* can offer an idea in a meeting and no one responds—yet a little while later, a *man* says the exact same thing that I said, everyone lights up and says it's a terrific idea?"

For me, Megan captured the frustration women have with this issue better than anyone when she told me about her experience at work:

*"I tend to be outnumbered by guys at group meetings. But I'll give my input, and nothing happens. Then one of my peers—say, Tom—paraphrases my idea. All of a sudden Tom's a hero. The rest of the guys start saying things like 'To Tom's point...' or 'As Tom has suggested...' And I feel like screaming, 'Hello? Are you*

*deaf? Didn't I just I say the same thing? Hello, hello, hello!' And there is no doubt they heard me. I speak clearly, loudly, and I still get ignored. Suddenly, Tom speaks and it's like someone fixed the generator and the lights come on. Then all of the guys are slapping Tom on the back and saying 'Hey Tom, you're the man!' It just gets old. It's like I am invisible. Why do I not get acknowledged for my thought leadership? How can you ever correct that?"*

I call this scenario the "incredible invisible woman" because, as Megan said, women tend to feel that no one can see or hear them when they attempt to contribute to a group discussion. (Believe it or not, some men also experience the same problem.) Here are some tips that will get your ideas heard:

**Emphasize the Visual; Minimize the Verbal:**
Men are overwhelmed by verbal input (remember Chapter 2), and they tend to pay less attention to it than they do to visual cues. To capitalize on this tendency, use the whiteboard or flipchart in the conference room. Or, if the room doesn't have one, bring a one with you when you head into a meeting. (You can also use a large notepad in a pinch.) That way, if you have an idea that you want to contribute to the discussion, you can write it on the board and point to it up for the group to see. Then, if someone mentions your idea later, you can always point back to the board and say something like: "I'm glad you agree with my idea!" or "As I said earlier." Make your thoughts and ideas visual; use whiteboard, overheads, writing, etc. Men are visual.

Once Karen saw the importance of "putting it in writing," she began implementing this idea and became more effective at work. "I remember being at a meeting where there were two males and two females in the room," she told me. "The other woman and I were saying virtually the same thing as one of the men—but the director, the other male, wasn't getting it from us. So the man stood up and wrote out the idea on a board in the meeting room and the director understood it better. What I learned from that—and what I've started doing myself—are two lessons: First, the guy was active. He got up and moved around. Second, he put it in writing. He gave a visual aid, and that sunk in better than all of our words."

## Pay Attention to the Timing

Comedians live by the motto, "It's all in the timing." That truism is one that you may want to adopt also, because, when it comes to getting an idea across in a meeting, your timing makes all the difference. When men get together, they spend a certain amount of time posturing for status—joking, one-upping each other (Chapter 3). Don't try to interrupt this process and don't throw out your ideas when men are in the middle of it. Wait. Watch their body language. When things have quieted down, say: "I have an idea, and I would like your input." Then **wait for them to stop and listen.** Once you're sure you have their attention, present your idea—and, if at all possible, put it in writing or use a visual cue as suggested in the previous section. Women sometimes want to "get down to business" at the beginning of a meeting—before the men have finished establishing their hierarchy. If you can resist that urge to "get started" in a meeting, then you will have a better chance of being heard.

## Think Fast; Talk Slowly

With all the connections in that intuitive, multi-tasking female brain of yours, you can often see solutions to problems rather quickly. And your "holistic," global thinking style also gives you the big picture in a way that a man's linear thought process generally does not. As a result, you may be the first one in a meeting to come up with a great idea or the perfect approach for a new business opportunity. But, as noted above, timing is everything. If you blurt out the idea as soon as it pops into your head—without considering your audience's attention level—your words may fall on deaf ears.

On top of that, you can also be blindsided by your own female tendency for collaboration. What I mean by this is: You may enter a meeting thinking that everyone will be offering their creative input so the group can come up with the best idea. That's the inclusive, "win-win" way. But remember, with a predominantly male group, you are speaking into a hierarchical system designed around the game of "I win, you lose." It's not that men and women can't collaborate—they can and often do. But if you've been frustrated by not having your ideas recognized, perhaps you need to pay attention to what type of meeting you're in and act accordingly. If you're in a creative, brainstorming session with co-workers of equal rank, then it's much more likely that you can toss around ideas and no one will try to take credit or ignore your suggestions. If it's a high-stakes session with the CEO, assume that the males in the room will all be fighting for status and you'll have to be more strategic about how you give your input.

One more thing about your mental process that you need to remember is this: Women sometimes need to verbalize in order to clarify their thoughts. There's nothing wrong with thinking out loud. You just need to know, however, that men generally don't do that and they may judge you as someone who "talks in circles" instead of getting to the point. If you absolutely must talk out your ideas, do so with trusted co-workers before or after the meeting. Or, if an idea comes to mind during the meeting, scribble it down first before saying it aloud.

Tricia found the suggestion to "think fast, talk slowly" to be particularly valuable for women struggling to get their ideas across. "I think women problem-solve much faster than men," she says. "The woman may already have seen the solution in her mind and, meanwhile, the guys are still jockeying for position. But then we women don't hold onto our ideas and present them at the right time, so they get lost."

"We forget that men think in a linear way," she adds. "In our way of thinking, we may have already arrived at the end point—but we don't give them the step-by-step data to take them there with us. Sometimes, you have to back up and walk someone through your idea one stage at a time, instead of making those intuitive leaps out loud and expecting them to leap with you." (Remember The PAPER Method™ from Chapter 2: Present one idea, get agreement, pause and then go to the next idea.)

When she speaks up in a meeting, Tricia also interjects a few phrases that remind her listeners of any ideas she's already offered, for example: "… as I said before," or "What I said earlier that we haven't finished addressing is this…"

"I keep going back to my point," Tricia says, "and I subtly emphasize that it's something I've already laid out on the table."

"If you can keep the thread of your idea going," she adds, "then you can build on it and get the recognition you deserve."

Notice that Tricia did not give up anything by making a concerted effort to highlight her ideas. She simply adapted her communication style to more closely match the thinking process of the men in her company, and, she reports, they have become much more receptive to her since she's done that. (Fact: men prize people of action. Don't be afraid to toot your horn, to say that YOU have a GREAT idea and they should stop and listen. Remember the power of the silent pause. Use it. *That's what men do.*

## Send the Right Signal

If you've ever watched a professional baseball game, you may have noticed that the pitcher and catcher communicate through hand signals. Sometimes, too, you'll see the manager touching his cap in a certain way to let the outfield know they need to back up, or to get the shortstop to move in. Quietly and efficiently, the men on the team recognize what these motions mean, and without speaking a word, they react accordingly.

You, too, send signals through your body language—but you may not always be aware of how you're delivering your message. And, just as getting the kid-glove treatment or being the "invisible" woman can prevent you from making the team, you, too, can you be sabotaged by your own lack of awareness about how you appear to others.

If I could offer you only one piece of advice about how to adjust your body language to improve communication with men at work, it would be this:

## Stop Fidgeting!

Not to sound like the nuns I remember from catechism class as a boy, but you have to "stop fidgeting." No joke.

When it comes to being taken seriously as a professional woman, keep this equation in mind: Less movement = more power.

Let me give you some evidence to prove this equation. Some time ago, a study was done about perceptions of power and authority. In the study, men and women were told to watch the start of a business meeting containing both male and female actors via closed circuit television. The study group was asked to select the people who they believed had the most power in the meeting. Because there was no sound, the observers had to get their cues from the body language of the actors. In all cases, both men and women tended to consistently select the same actors as the most powerful. Can you guess what criteria they used? It was movement. The actors, both male and female, who moved the *least* during the meeting, were seen as having the most power!

This makes perfect sense. A person who is self assured and in control is usually very deliberate in his or her movements.

Those who are unsure often dissipate their nervousness through excess movement and fidgeting.

Because of the high importance women place on relationships and collaboration, they tend to use excess movements—even when they feel more confident than men. In fact, in that study, the women averaged 27 distinct movements vs. the 12 for men. The moral is: Limit your movements.

For example, when you arrive for an important meeting, take your seat, open your notebook and sit back in a relaxed position. That posture sends an unconscious message to others in the room that you "have your stuff" together. Try it and have fun with it! Use this exercise to see for yourself how body language affects perceptions.

## EXERCISE: Cool Moves

*Instructions:* In meetings, practice watching other people who are considered powerful and in charge. Notice their posture. Watch how they move and gesture. Listen to how they speak. Use the space below to record your findings

---

---

---

---

---

---

---

---

---

---

**Your Turn:**
See if you can limit your movements in meetings and notice any differences in the way others treat you. Note your observations here:

_____

_____

_____

_____

_____

_____

_____

_____

_____

Although you may see the benefit of reducing your movements during important interactions, old habits are sometimes hard to break. Perhaps you can keep in mind the experience of my client, Dianne, to help you stay aware of your body language. I worked with Dianne before she went into an interview with a very prestigious and male-dominated firm. There were three other very qualified candidates, all male, vying for the same job. Everyone was told they would go through two rounds of interviews. To prepare for the interview, I had Dianne practice limiting her movements (and slowing her rate of speech, which was very fast). She called me after the interview to tell me that she was offered the job at the first interview! The manager told her that she projected the confidence and ability they wanted, and they felt there was no need to look further. And Dianne's story is only one of many such successes among women I've worked with or heard about who have learned the power of being still.

## Being a Team Player

One of the primary goals for improving your communication skills with men is for you to land a spot on the team—and even to lead it. Unfortunately, many of the team participation skills that come naturally to men are sometimes foreign to women. Plus, some women have had to struggle in isolation to rise through the corporate ranks, and that can make them wary of giving up any of the ground they've fought hard to win. During one of my seminars, Jillian brought up her struggle with letting down her guard to become a team player. "Women have a hard time laying down the sword," she said, "because we're wired to take care of the house and family as individuals. Men know they can get what they want and need by being on teams, but we're not wired that way."

While acknowledging the difficulties she faced, I pointed out to Jillian the benefits of re-framing her attitude. After we worked together, she began adjusting her communication style to be less combative and more team-oriented. When she started work at a new company, she decided to put into practice some of the skills she learned about asking to be included in decision-making sessions, timing the input of her ideas, and paying attention to her body language. Consequently, she became much more successful—and far less stressed—at work. She shared some of her observations with me and I'll let her have the last word here, because I couldn't have said it better myself:

*"I finally realized that men just want to win the game. If you can help them understand how they play a role in winning the game, in helping the whole team win, they'll get on board and align behind you."*

## BRAIN BASICS: Oxytocin and Vasopressin

Oxytocin is a hormone that plays an important role during labor and childbirth. It is considered the "primary bonding hormone" that links mother and child. Men have less of it in their bodies than women do—which may help boys to break the bond with their mothers when they are between the ages of four and six. While this task is difficult, boys have to take on this challenge in order to establish their identities as males, and that is when they begin pursuing bonds with other males. The neurochemical vasopressin is the male counterpart to oxytocin and it is linked not only to male bonding but also to guarding and defending behaviors.

### *They'll eat you alive...*

Ellen worked in Silicon Valley and her position in the company changed when it went through a re-organization. While she had previously worked with people on the sales side of the business, her new job required her to interact primarily with engineers on the service side. And, she also took on a lead role in implementing a major change in the type of services offered to high paying customers.

"Admittedly," says Ellen, "I was new to the services support group, and not an engineer. But when I presented the benefits of the new plan to the organization, I was put on the chopping block, torn to pieces!"

"I told them I had a vision," she says, "I knew this was tough, but we would get through it. They told me I didn't understand the business and I added no value because I was a 'business person' and not an engineer. Even though management supported what I was doing, many of the engineers had been 'born and raised' in that part of the company and they felt I was an outsider who came in and didn't really understand the customers' needs."

Ellen persisted, however, and kept standing up for the new program and her belief in it. Eventually, some members of the group—especially those who had originally been critical—admitted to her that they realized she had a much harder job than they thought she had. "They told me they admired me for not letting them wear me down," Ellen says. "I realized that in the culture of man to man, they are just as hard on one another. Very competitive. They would treat ANYONE that way. It wasn't that I was a woman."

"Women think they are being targeted," she adds, "but men do it to each other all the time. Many of these guys had been through the wringer and failed. Basically, if you fall apart, they will eat you alive. I tell the women I know that the minute they take it personally they're in trouble. They need to get out of that mindset. Working with men is just like dealing with another culture. You have to find out how they operate and vary your communication to get the outcomes you want as you would when dealing with someone from another country. It is no different with men; they really do have a different culture!"

## Chapter 9: You *Can* Be Heard!

Walking into the conference room for a job interview, I picked the chair at the head of the table and sat down. As Linda, the sales manager, asked about my background and experience, I responded with answers that were as direct and succinct as I could make them. Linda was looking to fill the last spot on her team, which, it turned out, was made up of all women. Unfortunately, she didn't pick me for that position. I didn't make the cut.

Then, not long after getting that news, I happened to run into Linda at a business function and I asked her about the interview. To her credit, she was honest with me. She told me that she felt I was too direct and that my presence would be too disruptive for her team.

That incident happened early in my career, and looking back, I can certainly understand how she could have felt that way. I probably *was* a little too blunt during the interview. It was my fault. At the time, I didn't appreciate the differences in communication styles between men and women. Consequently, I assumed that everyone saw the world as I did and acted accordingly. I reacted and responded to Linda just as though a man was doing the hiring. I gave short, direct answers instead of recognizing the importance of warming up my tone. I sat in the "power chair" at the top of the table because I assumed that would signal my strength and confidence. Little did I realize then that my words and actions were having the opposite effect from what I intended.

People who know me would say that I am very easy to work with (really!) and that Linda's interpretation of my style was completely off base. While it's nice to have support from your friends, the lesson I drew from the experience was that I did not adapt my communication style to Linda's—so I was judged according to her view of the world and the unconscious rules underpinning that view.

Though I went on to find a lucrative job after being turned down by Linda, my experience with her spurred me to start investigating more productive communication strategies. I began to see that it's *my* job, as it is yours, to appreciate the fact that each person, each culture, and each gender, has its own unique perception of reality. And we must adjust our style to fit that of the people we are communicating with if we want to be effective…if we want to be heard.

Throughout this book—and in fact, throughout my business—my aim is to provide the tools that can help both women and men work together effortlessly.

That is one of the reasons I named my company Diamond Dynamic. It is a metaphor for what can happen when the unique and complementary styles and behaviors of men and women are understood, appreciated and aligned within today's companies.

Let me tell you why I chose the diamond, specifically, to illustrate this metaphor and how that image may help you, too, as you hone your ability to work with men.

As you may remember from high school chemistry class, a diamond is made from the common carbon atom—the same atom found in coal and the lead in your pencil. The only difference between a piece of coal and a diamond is the way the carbon atoms are lined up.

In a piece of coal, the molecules are random, misaligned and unsupportive of one another. Each atom is weakly connected to its neighbor.

The molecules in the diamond, however, are configured in what science calls an *isometric-hexoctahedral* crystal lattice, which produces the most beautiful, enduring, and desirable substance on earth. Why? Because in a diamond the atoms are aligned and fully support one another. Unlike the atoms in a piece of coal, those in a diamond are cohesive rather than scattered. So if you look at what happens when men and women are able to communicate clearly, you'll see their work meshes elegantly, just like the atoms in a diamond— that's the "diamond dynamic."

Of course, not all diamonds are perfect. There are areas where the atoms do not fall precisely in line, and that produces a flaw, which makes the diamond less desirable. Too many of these flaws and the diamond might as well be a lump of coal—because when the atoms are not in their proper places in the crystal lattice, the stone loses is durability and desirability.

The same is true of modern companies. Some are well aligned and produce brilliant results for customers, employees and stockholders. Others are flawed. They are not aligned and produce only disappointment for clients and the people who own stock in them. The employees of such a company—the "atoms" if you will—are unhappy and they become alienated from the people they work with. Stress levels rise, motivation declines and the company becomes flawed, sometimes fatally. These flaws occur when there is a disconnect in the communication between employees—especially with male and female employees.

And when the level of communication within a company is low—combined with a lack of advancement opportunities, mentoring, or appreciation—women start heading for the exits. They become part of the so-called "Jane Drain," in which women drop out of the workforce, switch companies, or start their own businesses. This situation creates winners and losers. The winners are obviously those who create their own jobs and thrive. The losers, however, are the ones who don't make it and the companies who lose great talent.

For corporations, losing good people is always a blow. And in the face of global competition, they cannot afford to miss out on the creativity, innovation, and ability to collaborate that so many women have to offer.

And what about you, as an individual? You can lose, too, when your career choices are made in reaction to negative conditions rather than pro-active decisions that help you advance. It's one thing to leave your company because you are truly ready to go, or because a better offer comes along. But I hate to see any woman forced into career moves she would rather not make—especially when she makes those moves out of frustration over communication issues with men. So one of my goals has been to give you information that can help you reduce that level of frustration.

## We Can't Do It Without You

As I said in the Introduction, the purpose of this book is to make you a more effective communicator. Throughout these pages, you've learned about the primal forces that drive men's behavior; the differences in male and female brains that cause misunderstandings; and the unwritten rules of male business culture that might create obstacles in your path. I trust you've also learned a number of new strategies for dealing with these issues—and that you've been inspired by the successful women who so generously shared their workplace experiences.

You have an incredible amount to offer. As a woman, you already know more about the power of collaboration and empowerment than any man ever will.

Of course men will say that they want to empower people. They are all for collaboration. But I can tell you that deep down we do not understand those concepts the way women do. I am not saying that men don't intellectually want these things, we do. However it is not in our DNA the way it is for women. We are wired for competition and status, not collaboration and empowerment. In times of stress we will revert to our primal instincts!

This is not true of women. You are wired for collaboration and empowerment. In times of stress you know how to keep the group together, to include everyone. Companies desperately need you if they are going to survive in these challenging times.

Let's face it. The major source of value in today's corporations is its IP, Intellectual Property. That is, its innovation. Most everything else is outsourced. And how do companies maintain their competitive edge? Through their employees. And if those employees are unhappy or feel disenfranchised, what happens? They leave, or worse, they just keep quiet and do the bare minimum until something better comes along.

We need to hear your voice. You can be the one who helps align the "atoms" in a company that can change it from being a mere lump of carbon into a sparkling, enduring and precious diamond. I would like to end with a beautiful passage from Marianne Williamson's book: *"A Return to Love"* that captures the essence of what happens when you step forward and demand to be heard:

*Our deepest fear is not that we are inadequate. Our deepest fear is that we are powerful beyond measure. It is our light, not our darkness that most frightens us. We ask ourselves, 'Who am I to be brilliant, gorgeous, talented, and famous?'*

*Actually, who are you not to be? You are a child of God. Your playing small does not serve the world. There is nothing enlightened about shrinking so that other people won't feel insecure around you. We are all meant to shine, as children do. We were born to make manifest the glory of God that is within us.*

*It is not just in some of us; it is in everyone. And as we let our own light shine, we unconsciously give other people permission to do the same. As we are liberated from our own fear, our presence automatically liberates others.*

It is my hope that through the pages of this book you have learned a simple truth:

You *can* be heard.

And we can't wait to find out what you have to say!

# Appendix

# The Diamond Dynamic™

*If Someone Loses...*
*What's the problem!*

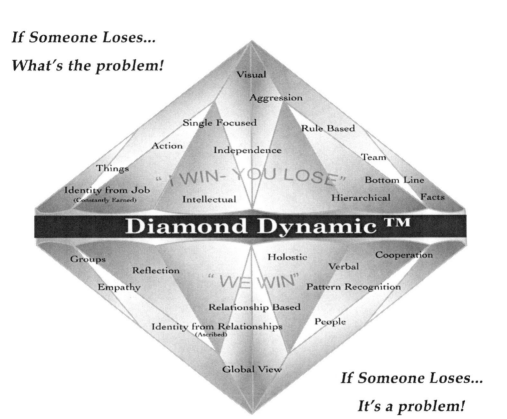

*If Someone Loses...*
*It's a problem!*

# Brain

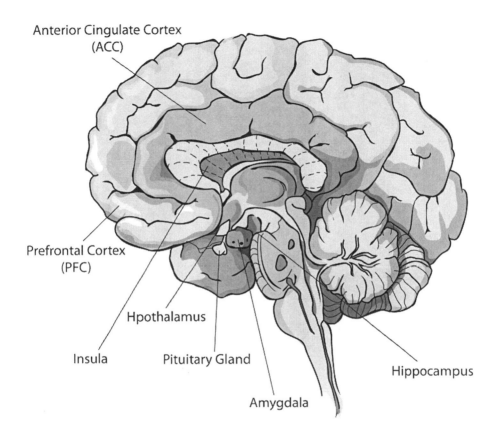

Anterior Cingulate Cortex
(ACC)

Prefrontal Cortex
(PFC)

Hpothalamus

Insula

Pituitary Gland

Amygdala

Hippocampus

# Bonus Offer

## Here's How to Get Your
## FREE SPECIAL BONUS:

*"The 3 Secret Principles That Govern Men's Lives"*

(Not Available To the General Public)

Have you ever wondered:
- **Why men seem to ignore you?**
- **Tell you "not to worry" about something that is bothering you?**
- **Forget about an argument you had a short time ago?**

In the *3 Secret Principles that Government Men's Lives* you will learn the three unconscious primal drives that have been hardwired into men's brains by Nature.

Get your free copy by going to
www.Diamond-Dynamic.com\3sp

# Contact Us

**Need**
- Speaker?
- Workshop?
- Consulting?
- Just Have a Question?

**We have a variety of offerings in**
- Influencing and Communication Skills
- Generational Communication
- Advance Listening and Questioning Skills
- Confidence Strengthening
- Reading Nonverbal cues (Body Language)
- Stress Management and Resilience

For more information about how we may be of service to you and your company, please call or email us for more information at:

- **Email:** info@Diamond-Dynamic.com
- **Website:** www.Diamond-dynamic.com
- **Tel:** 831.688.6811

**Michael Johnson**, founder of Diamond Dynamic (www.Diamond-Dynamic.com) helps corporations profit though understanding the world's two most diverse cultures: male and female.

Although biologically wired to think like a man, raising two daughters forced him to see the world through the eyes of women and fostered Mike's interest in gender communication. Today's his daughters enjoy successful careers in two male-dominated occupations; law enforcement Sheriff and professional chef.

Prior to starting his own business communication consulting firm, Mike enjoyed a successful sales career with General Electric and was recruited to develop and teach training and communication courses for GE employees.

Mike now lectures for San Jose State College of Business, UCSC and the Haas Graduate School of Business at U.C. Berkeley on entrepreneurship and is on the board of the Association for Corporate Growth and a member of Boardroom Bound, an organization dedicated to assisting women in preparing for and obtaining board positions in corporate America. He is also a mentor for Astia, a non-profit helping women-owned businesses obtain funding.

Mike has been featured in INC Magazine, Sales & Marketing Management, San Jose Business Journal, the San Jose Mercury News and the Santa Cruz Sentinel. Mike holds advanced certifications in Neuropsychology, Linguistics and Hypnotherapy and is coauthor of "Getting the Business Breakthrough You Want."

Mike Johnson can be reached at
www.Diamond-Dynamic.com or emailed at
mike@Diamond-Dynamic.com

# BUY A SHARE OF THE FUTURE IN YOUR COMMUNITY

These certificates make great holiday, graduation and birthday gifts that can be personalized with the recipient's name. The cost of one S.H.A.R.E. or one square foot is $54.17. The personalized certificate is suitable for framing and will state the number of shares purchased and the amount of each share, as well as the recipient's name. The home that you participate in "building" will last for many years and will continue to grow in value.

**Here is a sample SHARE certificate:**

HABITAT FOR HUMANITY

THIS CERTIFIES THAT

**YOUR NAME HERE**

HAS INVESTED IN A HOME FOR A DESERVING FAMILY

1985-2005

TWENTY YEARS OF BUILDING FUTURES IN OUR COMMUNITY ONE HOME AT A TIME

1200 SQUARE FOOT HOUSE @ $65,000 = $54.17 PER SQUARE FOOT
This certificate represents a tax deductible donation. It has no cash value.

## YES, I WOULD LIKE TO HELP!

*I support the work that Habitat for Humanity does and I want to be part of the excitement! As a donor, I will receive periodic updates on your construction activities but, more importantly, I know my gift will help a family in our community realize the dream of homeownership. **I would like to SHARE in your efforts against substandard housing in my community!** (Please print below)*

PLEASE SEND ME _____ SHARES at $54.17 EACH = $ $_____

*In Honor Of:* _____

*Occasion: (Circle One)*    HOLIDAY    BIRTHDAY    ANNIVERSARY

      *OTHER:* _____

*Address of Recipient:* _____

*Gift From:* _____ *Donor Address:* _____

*Donor Email:* _____

I AM ENCLOSING A CHECK FOR $ $_____ PAYABLE TO HABITAT FOR HUMANITY <u>OR</u> PLEASE CHARGE MY VISA OR MASTERCARD *(CIRCLE ONE)*

Card Number _____ Expiration Date: _____

Name as it appears on Credit Card _____ Charge Amount $ _____

Signature _____

Billing Address _____

Telephone # Day _____ Eve _____

**PLEASE NOTE:** Your contribution is tax-deductible to the fullest extent allowed by law.
**Habitat for Humanity • P.O. Box 1443 • Newport News, VA 23601 • 757-596-5553**
**www.HelpHabitatforHumanity.org**

LaVergne, TN USA
10 September 2010
196614LV00003B/15/P